EMPLOYMENT LAW

EMPLOYMENT LAW

University of
South Wales
Prifysgol
De Cymru

Library Services

**Elizabeth
Aylott**

KoganPage

LONDON PHILADELPHIA NEW DELHI

Publisher's note

Every possible effort has been made to ensure that the information contained in this book is accurate at the time of going to press, and the publishers and author cannot accept responsibility for any errors or omissions, however caused. No responsibility for loss or damage occasioned to any person acting, or refraining from action, as a result of the material in this publication can be accepted by the editor, the publisher or the author.

First published in Great Britain and the United States in 2014 by Kogan Page Limited

2nd Floor, 45 Gee Street	1518 Walnut Street, Suite 1100	4737/23 Ansari Road
London EC1V 3RS	Philadelphia PA 19102	Daryaganj
United Kingdom	USA	New Delhi 110002
www.koganpage.com		India

© Elizabeth Aylott, 2014

The right of Elizabeth Aylott to be identified as the author of this work has been asserted by her in accordance with the Copyright, Designs and Patents Act 1988.

ISBN   978 0 7494 6974 0
E-ISBN   978 0 7494 6975 7

British Library Cataloguing-in-Publication Data

A CIP record for this book is available from the British Library.

Typeset by Graphicraft Limited, Hong Kong
Print production managed by Jellyfish
Printed and bound by CPI Group (UK) Ltd, Croydon CR0 4YY

CONTENTS

ACKNOWLEDGEMENTS

With love to my boys; along with others I am privileged to share some very small part of your lives as you build your future.

To Jack, Jacob and Sam.

Introduction

The pace of change of legislation makes it difficult for both employers and employees to keep up to date with their rights and responsibilities in the business world. The general public view Employment Tribunals through the eyes of the media. Employees read about changes to employment law that reduce their rights or make it harder to claim at Employment Tribunals and they see Trade Unions challenging employment law in the courts. Employers read about employees who have taken discrimination cases winning large sums, and fear the cost of Employment Tribunals. Neither employees nor employers have a clear perspective of employment law.

This is the environment in which human resources (HR) professionals practice. We, as HR professionals, support line managers and senior managers to apply the law in our day-to-day work, and through the policies and procedures of the company we apply law to support employees to gain their rights and understand their responsibilities. With our up-to-date advice and our attempts to support the company to build an atmosphere of trust, we protect the company from Employment Tribunal claims. If there are claims we may find that we are involved in gathering evidence for the company's lawyer and may be called as a witness for the company, to give an account of our involvement in the case.

It is the HR professional who is viewed by the company as the expert in employment law, and it is a heavy responsibility. This book has been written to help HR professionals to build their expertise in order to support both employers and employees.

Aims of the book

This book has been developed with its primary focus on the need for HR professionals to understand and apply law, rather than a review of statute and case law. It provides a practical understanding of fundamentals of employment law for those of us new to the profession, whether we are an HR generalist, working in employment relations or taking up a new role as an employment law specialist. It focuses on the law that is relevant to an HR professional and so covers employment law for those working without Trade Unions and, as many HR generalists may have some health and safety responsibility, we also review health and safety legislation.

Employers that work without Trade Unions need to relate more closely with employees. For those employers that have recognized Trade Unions there is a main body that acts as representative for the employees and the HR professional may be responsible for supporting line managers:

- involved in collective bargaining, negotiating pay increases and other collective changes to terms and conditions;
- in negotiating variations of contracts with the Trade Union, rather than individuals;
- in providing collective involvement and participation methods which include the Trade Union;
- in managing discipline and grievance procedures with Trade Union representatives.

Some of the practicalities of working with Trade Unions are to be found in the companion book in this series, *HR Fundamentals: Employee Relations*.

The book has also been written for those studying CIPD courses, and in particular the content of the Level 5 Intermediate Certificate in HRM or the Level 5 Apprenticeship scheme. It covers the learning outcomes of these two courses and you will find the content mapped across to the chapters in Table 0.1. The book is not written to support Level 7 (Masters Level) courses with employment law content, but could be used as pre-reading to introduce students to the subject prior to commencing a Masters Level course.

It is important to stress that this book should be read together with its companion book, *HR Fundamentals: Employee Relations*. Discipline and grievance procedures are covered in detail in the companion book, along with dismissal and constructive dismissal. This is because these areas of HR practice are basic to employee relations and indicate the link between understanding pure employment law as a lawyer and applying law in HR practice.

TABLE 0.1 Cross mapping of content of CIPD Level 5 courses

CIPD Learning Outcomes Intermediate Level Certificate in HRM	CIPD Learning Outcomes for Level 5 Diploma in applied HRM – Higher Apprenticeship	Topics	Found in chapter
1. Understand the purpose of employment regulation and the way it is enforced in practice.	1. Understand the purpose of employment regulation and the way it is enforced.	The sources of domestic and European law; The relevant structure of the Civil Courts and Employment Tribunal system; The role of law in distributing social justice and ensuring fairness; The effect of regulation on the economy, employees, employers and society; The Employment Tribunal process and out-of-court settlements.	1
		The support employers may gain by following the law; The way in which employers may keep up to date with both statute and case law.	2
		The changing legal and moral framework for employers; Approaches to business strategy and compliance with the law; The issues and challenges that occur at different stages in the business lifecycle.	3
		Settlement agreements.	5
2. Know how to manage recruitment and selection activities lawfully.	2. Know how to manage recruitment and selection activities lawfully.	Implied and express rights in the contract; Written statement of particulars.	2
		Preventing discrimination in recruitment; Occupational requirements; Positive action; Immigration and employment; Temporary workers and the Agency Workers Regulations 2010; Establishing contracts; Discrimination – direct and indirect.	4
		Employment status.	5
		Short-listing.	6

TABLE 0.1 *continued*

CIPD Learning Outcomes Intermediate Level Certificate in HRM	CIPD Learning Outcomes for Level 5 Diploma in applied HRM – Higher Apprenticeship	Topics	Found in chapter
3. Know how to manage change and reorganization lawfully.	3. Know how to manage change and reorganization lawfully.	Multi-nation corporation and regulation.	3
		Changing contracts: flexibility clauses; Business transfers and the Transfer of Undertaking (Protection of Employment) Regulations 2006; Redundancy; Collective consultations.	4
		Changing contract – gaining consent; Communicating business transfers to stakeholders; Managing individual consultations.	5
		Changing contract – planning communication; Planning for replacement, retirement and succession planning; Planning for a programme of redundancies.	6
4. Know how to manage issues relating to pay and working time lawfully	4. Know how to manage issues relating to pay and working time lawfully.	Equal pay; Maternity, paternity and adoption rights; Parental leave; Time off for dependants; Flexible working requests; Working time; Minimum wage.	4
		Job Evaluation Schemes.	5
		'Keeping in Touch' days; Equal pay audits.	6
		Equal opportunities monitoring; Pay reviews.	7

TABLE 0.1 *continued*

CIPD Learning Outcomes Intermediate Level Certificate in HRM	CIPD Learning Outcomes for Level 5 Diploma in applied HRM – Higher Apprenticeship	Topics	Found in chapter
5. Be able to ensure that staff are treated lawfully when they are at work.	5. Be able to ensure that staff are treated lawfully when they are at work.	Right of association.	1
		Implied rights; Discrimination rights; Protecting employees during the employment relationship – discrimination; Unfair dismissal and Trade Union membership.	2
		Discrimination – the Equality Act 2010; Preventing discrimination during employment; Principles of health and safety.	4
		Challenging discrimination; Health and safety – getting advice and managing risks; Personal injury claims; Misconduct, gross misconduct, hearings and warnings.	5
		Establishing a diverse workforce; Health and safety training and reporting accidents and incidents; Well-being as part of absence management.	6
6. Know how to manage performance and disciplinary matters lawfully.	6. Know how to manage performance and disciplinary matters lawfully.	Dismissal rights; Misconduct and fair dismissal; Automatically unfair dismissal; Right to be accompanied; Introduction to whistle-blowing.	2
		Personal injury claims; Absence and capability; Whistle-blowing and discrimination.	5
		Whistle-blowing.	7

Structure of the book

This book introduces key themes which are then covered in more detail in the following chapters, with a focus on the application of law at the beginning of the employment relationship (during recruitment and selection), during the employment relationship and at the end of the employment relationship (at resignation, dismissal or redundancy).

In Chapter 1, we introduce the sources of law, the court system and Employment Tribunals. We examine the effect of legislation on the economy, employees, employers and society, and the role of legislation on the distribution of social justice. We review the Employment Tribunal process and out-of-court settlements.

In Chapter 2, we justify the need for employment law, for both employers and employees. We review the need of employees for a work–life balance, anti-discrimination practices and protection against unfair dismissal. We also review the support that employers gain by following the law. We look at the way in which employers may keep up to date with both statute and case law. In this chapter we introduce two areas of law – the contract and whistle-blowing.

In Chapter 3, we compare our ethical and moral framework, the values of the company and law, and look at when we might comply with the law and when it may be preferable to go beyond the minimum that the law demands. We examine the role of the HR professional and the impact of law for different business strategies and at different stages in the organization's lifecycle and our need to have the courage to challenge when necessary.

In Chapter 4, we review how the law works in practice, throughout the employment relationship, from recruitment and selection to dismissal. We examine discrimination legislation and the recruitment of workers from overseas and temporary staff. We look at changes in contracts and the law surrounding outsourcing and transferring in employees. We explore how to manage absence and health and safety. We review our role in ensuring equal pay and procedures for dealing with family friendly rights. Finally we explore the redundancy process.

In Chapter 5 we continue the practical theme throughout the employment relationship, examining how we work in practice in more detail. We clarify the issues surrounding the employment status of employees and look at how we gain consent to changes to employment contracts. We review how we might choose to communicate business transfers to stakeholders and, when problems occur, how we might arrange settlement agreements. We examine how short-term and long-term absence is managed and how we play a role in challenging discrimination. We look in more detail at both health and safety and maternity leave and pay, along with the practical issue of job evaluation. Finally at the end of the relationship, we explore how we might support employees facing redundancy.

In Chapter 6, we continue the practical theme by looking at particular issues in more detail. We go on to take a logical path from the beginning of the relationship at recruitment, through managing change and people, and terms and conditions, to the end of the employment relationship. We examine the risk of discrimination in short-listing, and discuss 'Keeping in Touch' days. We evaluate methods for reducing absence and assess the key points for carrying out an equal pay audit. We look at health and safety training, our legal responsibility to report accidents and incidents, review succession planning and the law, and finally investigate the support that can be provided for redundancy programmes.

In Chapter 7, we examine how we might measure the legal compliance of the company. This is a management of risk and is not solely reliant of the measurement of Employment Tribunal claims. We review some of the indicators of problems within the company – turnover and sickness absences, accidents and incidents all show problems with the way the organization is being run, not just compliance with employment law. We also explore the role of audits in reducing risk.

PART ONE

FUNDAMENTALS

What is employment law?

01

INTRODUCTION

Both employers and employees are protected by legislation, but to most people it is complex and confusing. This chapter seeks to introduce employment law, the court system and tribunals in an easy to understand manner. It also will discuss the reason for employment law and the effect of this law on all parties. In this chapter we will explore:

- the sources of domestic and European law;
- the relevant structure of the Civil Courts and the Employment Tribunal system;
- the role of law in distributing social justice and ensuring fairness;
- the effect of regulation on the economy, employees, employers and society;
- the Employment Tribunal process and out-of-court settlements.

Employment law

Employment law can be separated into three main themes:

- health and safety legislation;
- individual employment legislation;
- collective employment legislation.

The health and safety of workers has been ensured with a framework of legislation for many years, but this is not true of collective employment legislation which has been limited, with the UK preferring a voluntary approach. Employment law has moved from being based on common law to relying on statute. The extent of law covering these three main themes is vast and extends far beyond a book on the fundamentals of employment law. We will be focusing on individual employment law and touching on health and safety legislation.

Domestic law

The UK has a common law system. This means that judges have two main legal sources from which to make decisions; statute and common law.

Statute

A bill will pass through parliament, being discussed and amended at different stages in the process until it gains Royal Assent and becomes a statute. It is now primary law, and will be described as an Act of Parliament. Where necessary, statutes will allow for future regulations to be added and these are known as Statutory Instruments (SI). These Statutory Instruments ensure that additional detail or particular changes can be made to the Act without having to put the whole statute through Parliament. For example, the National Minimum Wage Act 1998 is updated by the National Minimum Wage (Amendment) Regulations 2008 (SI 2008/1894), whereby small amendments in wording have been made, and the National Minimum Wage (Amendment) Regulations 2012 (SI 2012/2397), whereby annual changes in the national minimum wage have been inserted into the regulations.

Case law

Over the years, judges have made decisions on cases that have become a binding precedent, as they have interpreted the law in a particular new way. It is not the actual decision that becomes binding but the reason for the decision which then can be applied to other similar cases: if the facts of the current case significantly resemble those of the precedent then it will be binding. Judges will interpret the facts of the case in light of any relevant case law and apply this to the case to support them in making their decision.

These precedent cases help by providing practical situations to which statute law has been applied. For example the Employment Rights Act 1996 provides information on the right not to be unfairly dismissed and the remedies for unfair dismissal but it is *British Homes Stores v Burchell* (1980) ICR 303, EAT which provides clarity on how to determine whether an unfair dismissal case has been managed correctly.

Courts higher in the hierarchy have precedent over the lower level courts. This means that decisions made at Supreme Court level take precedent over those made at Employment Appeal Tribunals or Employment Tribunals. This may become clearer if you look at Figure 1.1.

Codes of Practice

Codes of Practice have been particularly relevant in the education and support of employers to apply statute. The Advisory, Conciliation and Arbitration Service (Acas) has a duty to provide Codes of Practice '*as it thinks fit for the purpose of promoting the improvement of industrial relations*' (Trade Union and Labour Relations (Consolidation) Act 1992, s.199), and the Secretary of State also has the power to produce Codes of Practice, in consultation with Acas. The Commission for Equal and Human Rights (CEHR) and the Health and Safety Executive (HSE) can also produce Codes of Practice.

FIGURE 1.1 The Employment Tribunal system

European Court of Justice

Supreme Court

Court of Appeal

Employment Appeal Tribunal

Employment Tribunal

Employers that fail to abide by these Codes of Practice are not liable and therefore judges cannot base their decisions on the fact that these Codes of Practice have not been applied in the workplace. However judges are able to take the failure to adhere to a Code of Practice into account. This means that this factor may support other facts which lead judges to their decisions.

European law

As part of the European Union, the UK is subject to European law, with European law having supremacy and therefore superseding any domestic law. This means that domestic law should be consistent with European law. Article 288 of the Treaty on the Functioning of the European Union 2012/C 326/01 explains that the European Union will produce regulations, directives and decisions which may be dealt with differently by the member states. Regulations are to be taken in their entirety and will apply directly to the member states and are the equivalent of European Union Acts of Parliament. A directive can be interpreted into domestic law as it is less specific and most European Union influence on UK employment law has been through directives. Decisions may be provided for a specific member state, company or individual and is binding on them. Decisions are made by institutions such as the European Court of Justice.

For example, the Parental Leave Directive (96/34/EC) was implemented in the UK in 1999, as an amendment to the Employment Rights Act 1996. The rights are incorporated into the Act and the details placed in a Statutory Instrument, the Maternity and Parental Leave Regulations 1999 (SI 1999/3312). The Parental Leave Directive (96/34/EC) has now been repealed by the European Union and replaced by the Parental Leave Directive (2010/18/EC) with the rights remaining in the Employment Rights Act 1996 and the details found in the Statutory Instrument, the Parental Leave (EU Directive) Regulations 2013 (SI 2013/283). Here the UK has been able to apply its own interpretation of parental leave and the 2013 Regulations are as a result of consultation.

In context – social justice and fairness

We need to appreciate social justice and the approach of international bodies to social justice if we are to understand the reasoning behind legislation, rather than just how to apply the law. Social justice is the distribution of advantages and disadvantages within society and is based on equality and equal opportunity. It concerns aspects of citizenship, covering access to healthcare, education, justice and an acceptable standard of living. Within the workplace, social justice also refers to access to rights and fairness. For example, it refers to the right to influence decisions (employee voice) the right to justice (access to appeals) and protection against exploitation (fair distribution of pay and benefits). Social justice to some degree is supported by law.

The International Labour Organization promotes 'decent work' for all on an international scale and has agreed the principles of fundamental rights with its member states. These include:

- the right to association and collective bargaining;
- the elimination of child labour and all forced labour;
- the elimination of discrimination.

It sees work as being '*a source of personal dignity, family stability, peace in the community, democracies that deliver for people, and economic growth that expands opportunities for productive jobs and enterprise development*' (International Labour Organization, 2013a). This puts social justice on the employment agenda but these principles are only basic rights with little legal foundation. They are accepted through member country ratification and monitored by the International Labour Organization. The European Union has focused its social policy on the regulation of employment (Majone, 1993), establishing a set of minimum health and safety and employment rights for the member states which are formed through directives and regulations.

Whilst the International Labour Organization and European Union may be viewed as using their position solely to reduce poverty and social exclusion, it is argued by some academics that they may be protecting employment rights against the effects of competitiveness. Multinational companies can choose where best to site their businesses and the legal rights of employees play a part in this decision. They may choose to base their businesses in countries where their responsibilities to employees are less onerous, and it is easy both to hire and fire. This concept is known as 'social dumping' and according to Holland (1996), it is the protection of employees' rights from social dumping that has also influenced European Union policy. However this argument lacks some substance. When looking at the International Labour Organization's fundamental rights there is little evidence that those countries supporting these basic rights are any less competitive than those countries whose record on basic employment rights is poor (OECD, 1996).

So the law, whether domestic or European, protects the rights of the weaker party in the employment relationship. It ensures that rights are secured for all employees, not just distributed arbitrarily, dependent on the discretion or whim of an employer. It also ensures that all employees are treated equally.

However whilst law protects the weaker party we cannot assume that it reflects a moral stance. Whilst laws should follow natural justice, moral choices depend on the perspective of each individual and determining what is natural justice may be difficult. For example, in the UK not all employment rights are protected at the beginning of the employment relationship and the right to be protected from unfair dismissal can only be applied after two years' service (with some exceptions). Ethically it may be argued that this does not meet natural justice, as employers can dismiss employees without following any procedure. But in this case it enables employers to have greater flexibility and so encourages them to recruit new employees, reducing unemployment at a time of economic hardship.

The law and models of justice

In *HR Fundamentals: Employee Relations* (Aylott, 2014) we reviewed the four different types of justice and described them as follows:

- Distributive justice is the perceived fairness of the allocation of rewards.

- Procedural justice relates to the fairness of the procedures used, and employees evaluate the fairness against a number of criteria. These include the way in which the organization selects managers in the process, the method used to collect information, how decisions are made and whether there is access to an appeals process (Leventhal, 1980). An employee may perceive a procedure as unfair if there is no method to appeal a decision.

- Interactional justice relates to the relationship the manager has with the employee and fairness within the supervisory relationship. This could include the manager's dishonesty, invasion of the employee's privacy, disrespectful treatment and derogatory judgments (Bies, 2001). An employee may accept a low pay rise if given a clear explanation and treated with respect by his or her line manager.

- Informational justice refers to the transparency of information about the process. Some employers make sure all procedures are clearly explained on their intranet sites.

Employment legislation is specifically effective in the provision of distributive justice (for example, ensuring payment in lieu of remaining holiday pay at dismissal) and procedural justice (for example, the disciplinary procedure). The provision of interactional justice can be seen in the role of anti-discriminatory legislation.

In context – the effect of regulation

Regulation of the employment relationship will impact on employers, employees, the unemployed and society, and it can be argued that a non-regulated labour market would enable employees to compete on merit, purely the effect of supply and demand. In the UK, if we exclude health and safety legislation, for which there has been statute and case law for over 200 years, there has been little employment statute or case law and instead a history of voluntarism rather than law in relation to collective employee relations. This has changed, with the rights of employees becoming more than that of determining whether the contract has been breached, but instead has been reinforced as rights in statute, and collective employee relations have been given a solid legal framework.

When regulation is discussed it is the effect of employment protection legislation that is predominately referred to. Since 1946, when Stigler first argued against the minimum wage, the role of employment regulation has been viewed by traditional economists as detrimental. More recently, highly regulated employment protection has been shown to slow down the labour market, with employers retaining employees during a recession but not recruiting new employees for fear of problems when dismissing them later on. This therefore has little impact on unemployment levels but the lack of movement means that those who become unemployed may spend longer waiting to find another job (Blanchard and Landier, 2002). Some governments have provided partial regulation in some cases. For example, employment protection legislation makes it difficult for French employers to make employees redundant but with fixed-term contracts the severance pay is less. At the end of the fixed term, employees may be made redundant or become permanent staff. In the UK the application of unfair dismissal rights normally only commences after two years' service (with some exceptions). Blanchard and Landier (2002) believe that such partial protection is detrimental to employees and the labour market. They suggest that whilst it persuades employers to recruit, it also encourages them to dispense with staff while the cost is low and re-recruit a new employee.

One political argument is to reduce employment protection legislation to improve labour market flexibility and reduce the impact on long-term unemployment. However it is very difficult for a government to propose reduction or elimination of employment protection legislation. Such legislation protects existing employees in their jobs. If it remains difficult for employers to dismiss or make employees redundant then employees have greater bargaining power for better terms and conditions. Employment protection legislation provides employees with a degree of job security and, if employers are to retain their existing employees, enables these employees to develop their abilities and, in particular, access company-specific training. A stable and trained workforce enables the organization to be more competitive. This is because an employee with good job security will 'go the extra mile' and any resulting improved productivity matches any additional costs of legislation to the employer (Altman, 2000). In fact there is evidence that job security along with other high-commitment practices can improve business performance and competitiveness (Pffefer, 1998).

So despite the traditional economic argument against regulation, and the resultant effect on long-term unemployment, a degree of regulation is necessary to:

- meet political and social demands;
- provide a stable and engaged workforce;
- build competitive companies;
- sustain the economy.

CASE STUDY   Balancing employer flexibility and employee protection

The approach of the Confederation of British Industry to the legal framework for employment is to press for decreased regulation and increased flexibility. It recognizes a framework of basic employment rights, supporting for example anti-discrimination legislation and the national minimum wage (despite the traditional economist viewpoint taken by Stigler (1946)). The Confederation of British Industry argues that whilst basic rights support the labour market, certain legislation obstructs it (Confederation of British Industry, 2010). Some of the Confederation of British Industry's dispute is with the impact of European law on business and the need for clarity in both European Union and domestic law rather than costly and lengthy interpretation of law through the courts.

The Confederation of British Industry proposed a reduction of consultation from 90 days to 30 days for redundancies of 100 employees or over, in order to meet the need for certainty required by employees and employers alike. The Trade Union Congress (2012) resisted this change in employment protection, suggesting that a reduction would increase unemployment and damage jobs. Its research suggested that during the recession longer periods of consultation helped employers and unions find ways to reduce redundancies. However amendments to s.188 of the Trade Union and Labour Relations (Consolidation) Act 1992, which came into force in April 2013, have reduced consultation for 100 or more redundancies from 90 days to 45 days.

Other proposals by the Confederation of British Industry towards increased flexibility have centred on changes to collective legislation and, to support business, changes to the Employment Tribunal system. Whether these changes help support the weaker party in the employment relationship, the unemployed worker or help put British business on a firmer footing is yet to be seen.

The role of the court system

The court system provides a structure for cases to be heard and a system of appeal in order for parties to gain justice.

Civil and criminal law

Within the UK law there are two subdivisions, criminal and civil law, each with its own court system. Civil courts provide a way for claims to be made to compensate for loss. In general, employment cases fall under the civil law but some cases may have a criminal element and so may be prosecuted by the Crown Prosecution Service.

The role of courts in employment law

The majority of cases that affect employers and employees will be heard at an Employment Tribunal. If the Employment Tribunal has erred in its judgment on a question of law then the case can be referred to the

Employment Appeal Tribunal. Appeal can then be taken up to the Court of Appeal and the Supreme Court. This is the end of the process for domestic law, but if there is an issue of law that relates to the application of European law, then the case may be referred to the European Court of Justice (see Figure 1.1 earlier).

Cases of negligence are usually related to health and safety legislation. The Employment Tribunal does not have jurisdiction over negligence cases where there has been a breach of a duty of care with a resultant injury or loss. These tend to be heard at the High Court, Queen's Court Division, with the right of appeal to the Court of Appeal and the Supreme Court.

The role of tribunals in employment law

Employees that wish to make a claim do so by completing an ET1 form. Since 29 July 2013, most claimants have been required to pay a fee that is sent along with their ET1 claim. Those eligible to claim without paying a fee (who meet the disposable capital and gross monthly income tests) can claim a fee remission. The claim can be sent, delivered by hand or presented online, and payment of fees is by credit or debit card with online claims. Postal claims are now sent to a central office along with a cheque or postal order. Those claims presented by hand (along with the fee or fee remission application) must be delivered to the designated Employment Tribunal for that region.

The ET1 should be received by the Employment Tribunal normally within three months of the date of termination of the contract with the employer, or the last day that the employee worked for the employer prior to resigning (and claiming frustration of contract). There are special rules for time limits for redundancy and equal pay claims. Once the ET1 has been accepted by the Employment Tribunal, it will send the employer a copy of the ET1 and an ET3 form for them to complete. The ET3 must be received by the Employment Tribunal within 28 days. If the Employment Tribunal does not receive the ET3 it will make a default judgment. Once the ET3 is accepted by the Employment Tribunal, a copy is sent to the claimant and to Acas.

Structure of an Employment Tribunal

The Employment Tribunal consists of a judge and two lay members, one with experience of employee issues and the other employer issues. In practice this may mean that one tends to have Trade Union experience and the other HR experience, but this is not necessarily the case. The judge must have some legal qualification and at least five years' experience but may not necessarily be a solicitor or barrister, though the majority are.

Jurisdiction of Employment Tribunals

The Employment Tribunal has limited jurisdiction, which means that there are only certain issues that the Tribunal can hear. There is a wide range including:

- suffering a detriment, discrimination, including indirect discrimination, harassment or victimization or discrimination based on association or perception on grounds of age or other protected characteristics (Equality Act 2010, s.13, s.14, s.19, s.26, s.27, s.120);
- failure to pay equal pay for equal value work (Equality Act 2010, s.64, s.120, s.127, s.128);
- failure to consult for redundancy (Trade Union and Labour Relations (Consolidation) Act 1992, s.189);
- failure to receive a redundancy payment (Employment Rights Act 1996, ss. 163 and 177);
- failure of the employer to consult with an employee representative or Trade Union about a proposed transfer (Transfer of Undertakings (Protection of Employment) Regulations (SI 2006/246), r.12);
- the right to be accompanied – and there is detriment (Employment Relations Act 1999, ss. 11 and 12);
- failure of the employer to pay or an employer makes unauthorized deductions (Employment Rights Act 1996, s.23);
- failure to receive a written pay statement (Employment Rights Act 1996, s.11(2)).

Prior to the Employment Tribunal

Once the ET1 and ET3 forms are received, Acas will contact the claimant to determine whether they wish to use the Acas conciliation service. An increased requirement for early conciliation is expected to come into force in April 2014. Claimants will need to go through conciliation prior to making a claim. This starts with the claimant completing an Early Conciliation Form in order to commence conciliation with Acas. If conciliation does not resolve the issue, then the claimant will be issued with a certificate which shows that the process of early conciliation has been completed. This will be submitted with the ET1. The precise process of early conciliation and its relation to an Employment Tribunal ET1 claim is unclear at this stage. (For more details see Chapter 7.)

It is usual that a case management meeting is held with the judge, and any orders made by the judge will need to be complied with. To prepare for the case both parties may wish to gain more information from each other, and the Employment Tribunal may give orders for this. The date for the tribunal hearing will be received by both parties at least 14 days prior to the hearing. Each party may wish witnesses to attend and will need to send the bundle of documents to be used at the tribunal hearing to the other party, within seven days of the hearing. Table 1.1 shows the length of time taken for Employment Tribunal cases along with the average awards for the different jurisdictions.

At the hearing

It is not always necessary to have a legal representative – they will have an understanding of the process and law but there is a cost which may not be covered despite the fact that a respondent may win the case. Each side

TABLE 1.1   Employment Tribunal and Employment Appeal Tribunal Annual Statistics 2011–12 (Ministry of Justice, 2012)

Jurisdiction	Average award (all claims)	Average time in weeks (all single claims)
Age discrimination	£6,065	24
Disability discrimination	£8,928	29
Race discrimination	£5,259	30
Religious belief discrimination	£4,267	30
Sex discrimination	£6,746	27
Sexual orientation discrimination	£13,505	25
Unfair dismissal	£4,560	18

will be able to call witnesses, cross-examine witnesses and provide evidence themselves. Which party goes first will depend on the case, and the burden of proof required. For example, in unfair dismissals the employer will usually lead the proceedings, as they need to prove the dismissal was fair, whilst in discrimination cases the employee will usually start the proceedings, as it is necessary for them to prove that there may be discrimination. The employer would then need to provide an adequate explanation for their actions.

The case is heard, with both parties summing up their argument before the panel, or before the judge if the judge is sitting alone. Then the panel or the judge, withdraws to make the decision. If the judgment accepts the claimant's case then both parties will need to produce evidence and submissions that relate to the claimant's remedy. At times there are separate remedy hearings, but often evidence on remedy may be covered as part of the hearing or covered later in the hearing itself, if there is time. The respondent should therefore have prepared evidence. For most claims the claimant will be seeking compensation for loss of earnings and the respondent may be able to provide some evidence about how easy it would be for the claimant to find similar employment. However for unfair dismissal there is a possibility that the claimant may seek reinstatement or re-engagement. Very occasionally the Employment Tribunal may wish the respondent to provide the claimant with the same or similar job but the employer can prepare evidence in order to respond to this.

Out-of-court settlements

If an employer is in a dispute with an employee it is possible for the employer to instigate a 'without prejudice' conversation. This means that these discussions to agree a settlement cannot be used at Employment Tribunal. (It is now possible for employers to offer and discuss settlement even when a prior dispute between the employer and employee does not exist.)

An out-of-court settlement is when the claimant and respondent (employee and employer) come to an agreement about the dispute without resorting to redress through the Tribunal. This may be achieved through Acas or at any time prior to the Employment Tribunal. Previously known as a compromise agreement, it is a legally binding contract between an employer and employee, usually made during or after termination of the employment contract (for example, redundancy or dismissal). The legal framework for settlement agreements can be found in s.111A Employment Rights Act (1996) and is supported by a Code of Practice (Acas, 2013b) and additional guidance (Acas, 2013a).

Any discussion in order to make an out-of-court settlement is made 'without prejudice' which means that the discussion and any relevant papers are inadmissible as evidence at an Employment Tribunal. The rights discussed, and sometimes conceded, in a private discussion are only accepted as part of this discussion and not for any future litigation. Confidentiality must be maintained, but the right to this is lost if there is improper conduct, as described in the Code of Practice. So, for example, if during the seven days an employee considers the offer, the employer reduces the offer or the employee threatens to undermine the employer's reputation, then the status of 'without prejudice' is lost. Any document relating to the arrangement of a settlement should be recorded as 'without prejudice' (but only those documents truly part of an attempt towards a settlement will be included as 'without prejudice' despite the term). 'Without prejudice' allows these documents to take a privileged status.

Settlement agreements are generally used when there is an employment dispute but this is not necessarily the case. Settlement agreements can be used to protect the employer, at a cost, and are consensual and mutual agreements, with the employee able to reject a settlement agreement. Some employers choose to make all redundancies through settlement agreements, others do not, and sometimes they are used to manage an employee whose performance is unsatisfactory out of the organization. For whatever reason, settlement agreements are usually proposed by the employer and the employee should take legal advice so they can negotiate effectively. Often the consideration made by employers includes payment but also a job reference, helping the employee to find a new role.

There are some areas in which settlement agreements cannot be made. For example in cases of whistle-blowing or automatically unfair dismissal, the employer will not be able to make a payment to the employee. This is to protect the rights of employees.

Any payments made by means of a settlement agreement are tax exempt (up to £30,000) as are any legal costs (new provisions are being made to s.413A, Income Tax (Earnings and Pensions) Act (2003) to overcome these existing provisions).

Conclusion

In general, employers and employees alike do not want to resort to the law to resolve their differences. At times employers, particularly small employers, can feel that the extent of the law puts them at a disadvantage. Yet employment law is there to protect the weaker party, be that a junior member of the team being unfairly dismissed or a senior manager who is being made redundant. Not all employers have the interests of their employees in their sights when they are seeking to be profitable or struggling to survive. Not all employees act professionally and honestly and the law should protect both parties.

For several reasons the number of Tribunal cases has reduced, and the promotion of settlement agreements may support this reduction further. Hopefully some of this reduction is because of better HR practice, with employers following the law and employees less likely to resort to litigation but preferring to talk. The trend over the next few years will be telling.

In the next chapter we justify the need for employment law, for both employers and employees. We review the need of employees to a work–life balance, anti-discrimination practices and protection against unfair dismissal and the role of the law in supporting business reputation and good practice. However, we finish this chapter with a look at the trend for making Employment Tribunal claims.

CASE STUDY   Reviewing Tribunal claims

According to the *Daily Mail* (Doughty, 2013), the number of disgruntled employees seeking compensation at Employment Tribunals has dropped by more than a fifth in just two years. It is argued that claims have dropped from more than 235,000 in 2010 to 186,300 in 2011 as a result of the recession, low pay and poor job security. This is a drop of 21 per cent.

TABLE 1.2 Employment Tribunal and Employment Appeal Tribunal Annual Statistics 2011–12 (Ministry of Justice, 2012)

	2010–11	2011–12	Percentage change
Unfair dismissal	47,900	46,300	–3.34
Sex discrimination	18,300	10,800	–40.98
Working time directive	114,100	94,700	–17.00
Redundancy pay	16,000	14,700	–8.13
Redundancy – failure to consult	7,400	8,000	+8.11
Equal pay	34,600	28,800	–16.76
Race discrimination	5,000	4,800	–4.00
Transfer of undertaking – failure to consult	1,900	2,600	+36.84
Part-time regulations	1,600	770	–51.88
National minimum wage	520	510	–1.92
Discrimination on the grounds of religion or belief	880	940	+6.82
Discrimination on the grounds of sexual orientation	640	610	–4.89
Disability discrimination	7,200	7,770	+7.92

Sex discrimination claims were down by 41 per cent and equal pay Tribunal cases, the third most common claim, fell by 17 per cent. What is difficult to ascertain is whether this is because employees are anxious to avoid Tribunals and retain jobs when the cost of living is high and jobs difficult to find, or whether this is because employers' practices have improved. Certainly the number of Tribunal cases peaked in 2009–2010 and has been dropping since.

The Coalition has made significant changes to the Tribunal system to persuade employees to find other ways to resolve disputes, promoting Acas conciliation schemes and settlement agreements to prevent the need for litigation. Fees for taking an Employment Tribunal claim were introduced in the summer of 2013 with both a submission and a hearing fee. If employees make a claim, there is a deposit of £1,000 for claimants that take a weak case to Tribunal, and though costs are rarely awarded, there is the option for Tribunals to award costs up to £20,000 for claims viewed as spurious.

Tribunals have been amended to reduce the cost, both to the Government and employers. They have reduced the time spent at Tribunals by enabling witness statements to be taken as read. They have reduced the cost to Government by enabling judges to sit alone on unfair dismissal cases. The Government has collated figures that put the cost of an Employment Tribunal to employers at £6,200 (for claimants £1,800 and for the Exchequer, £3,200) (BIS – Department for Business, Innovation and Skills, 2013a).

For those claimants that are awarded their Employment Tribunal claim, since July 2013 there has been a cap of 52 weeks' pay or £74,000 (whichever is the lower) for an unfair dismissal claim.

Unfair dismissal cases were down over two years from 57,400 to 46,300 and sex discrimination claims from 18,200 to 10,800. Equal pay disputes taken to Tribunals dropped from 37,400 to 28,800 over two years, and race discrimination claims went down from 5,700 to 4,800.

According to the *Daily Mail* (Doughty, 2013) the average compensation award won by the employee in unfair dismissal cases was £4,560. In race discrimination cases it was £5,526, but the biggest award of the year went to hospital consultant Eva Michalak, who won £4.5 million for race and sex discrimination after she was bullied out of her job by colleagues.

The Employment Relations Minister Jo Swinson said: 'Employment tribunals are costly for everyone, in terms of money but also time and stress. Tribunals should be the last resort, not the first port of call.'

The importance of employment law

02

INTRODUCTION

Employment law ultimately protects employees from exploitation, but it also works towards good practice and encourages activities that will support business. In this chapter we justify the need for employment law for both employees and employers. This will also give us the opportunity to introduce the employment contract with its implied and express terms, the formal document on which, it can be argued, the employment relationship is based.

In this chapter we will explore:

- the needs of employees to a work–life balance, anti-discrimination practices and protection against unfair dismissal;
- the different implied contractual rights for employees and employers;
- the support employers may gain by following the law;
- the way in which employers may keep up to date with both statute and case law.

Protecting employees

We have already explained that employment law has a social justice role and that law exists essentially to maintain justice and to protect the weaker party, the employee. Since 1997, when the Labour Government was elected, there has been an increase in statutory employment rights, which though amended has not been wholly reversed by the Coalition Government. Employers' resistance to this change is also understandable as we have moved from a voluntarist to a legal approach to the employment relationship. Employers can accept the increased legislation surrounding health and safety but find it challenging to see a similar or even more extreme change to the moderation of the employment relationship, which has been in their sphere of control. However, these rights have some logical foundation which makes it easier for us as HR professionals to advise employers on their responsibilities. Examples of these rights are as follows (these are the primary employment rights but are not exclusive):

- work–life balance rights;
- discrimination rights;
- contractual rights;
- dismissal rights.

It is important to mention that, despite focusing on protecting employees and their rights, employees do also have responsibilities and duties towards their employers and examples of these implied duties are:

- to be obedient;
- to work in good faith;
- to adapt to new working methods;
- to use reasonable care and skill;
- to maintain confidentiality.

Work–life balance rights

Work–life balance rights provide employees with the ability to manage modern living. Most families are two wage earners in one guise or another. According to the OECD (2011) dual earners are most common in all European countries, a fairly radical change in this generation. However, it is more complex when the data are looked at in detail (see Table 2.1).

TABLE 2.1 Full-time working partners across USA, UK and European countries (OECD, 2011)

	USA	UK	OECD
Partners working full-time	61.8%	21.1%	39.7%

The figures in Table 2.1 demonstrate that partners in the USA tend to both work full-time. However, add in part-time working availability and there is a clear change. In the USA few partners choose to work part-time but in the UK 40 per cent of partners work, with one part-time and one full-time. This demonstrates a complex and differing range of needs when both the needs of employers and families are brought together, which the law attempts to reconcile and we apply when we receive flexible working requests on behalf of the employer. The work–life balance rights are as shown in Table 2.2.

TABLE 2.2 Work–life balance rights with relevant legislation

Right	Relevant legislation
Regulation of employment wages and hours	National Minimum Wage Act 1998 Working Time Regulations 1998
Maternity, paternity, and adoption pay and leave rights	A range of legislation including: Social Security Contributions and Benefits Act 1992 Employment Rights Act 1996 Employment Relations Act 1999 The Maternity and Parental Leave Amendment Regulations 2002 SI 2002/2789
Flexible working rights	Employment Act 2002 Work and Families Act 2006
Time off for dependants	Employment Relations Act 1999

Flexible working is covered in more detail in Chapters 4 and 6.

Discrimination rights

The UK has a history of ethnic diversity and this has increased in the twenty-first century: net non-British migration has generally been between 200,000 and 300,000 since 2002 and immigration of non-British citizens was at 439,000 in the six months between March and June 2012 (Office for National Statistics, 2013). This describes a movement of citizens, with a diversity of languages, values, backgrounds and religious affiliations. Add to this the speed of change and the concentration of different races in various locations, and this may lead to difficulties of social integration. It is from this picture of society that our employees of any ethic background are drawn.

We also see a society with an increase of older people, with 10 million people over 65 in the UK in 2010: this is one in six of the population and it is forecast that by 2050 it will be one in four (Cracknell, 2010). This both puts a pressure on working age employees (as their tax goes towards pensions) and the Government to finance support for the elderly, but more relevant to our discussion is the increase of older people in the workforce. The default retirement age has been removed, which means that employees no longer leave work at 65, but are free to work as long as they wish and are physically able to. The state retirement pension has been moving towards age 68 for those retiring in 2046 (Gov.UK, 2013a) which means that older people wishing to leave work before their state pension starts will need an appropriate private pension or savings to enable them to retire. This picture of an older population is mirrored across most other European countries (Cracknell, 2010).

Most of the research on the effects of discrimination are based on racial or gender discrimination, and has predominately been carried out in the USA. However this is likely to be transferable to other countries, and other people with different protected characteristics. For those wanting to work, perceived acts of discrimination can have serious adverse effects. Depression, anxiety and distress have been shown to result from perceived discrimination (Kessler *et al*, 1999) and perceived discrimination has also been associated with or is a potential risk factor for a range of physical health problems including high blood pressure, obesity, substance use and breast cancer (Williams and Mohammed, 2009). These findings should not come as a surprise as they describe individuals' attempts to cope with stress and the physical effects of stress. Discrimination is a stressor which individuals attempt

TABLE 2.3 Symptoms of stress

Emotional	Mental	Physical	Behaviour change
Depression or anxiety	Lack of concentration	Heart problems – palpitations and heart disease	Changes in eating habits
Increased emotional reactions	Confusion and indecision	Eczema and psoriasis	Increased smoking, drinking or drug taking
Loneliness, withdrawn	Poor memory	Musculoskeletal pains such as back pain	Changes in sleeping patterns
Loss of motivation commitment, self-esteem and confidence		Nausea and lack of appetite and, in the long term, ulcers	

to manage and the physiological responses to stress over time have poor health outcomes. Some of the symptoms of stress are shown in Table 2.3.

Many forms of stress at work can be managed, but it is the uncontrollable and unpredictable causes of stress which can have the most impact on health, and discrimination is both uncontrollable and unpredictable – so having support mechanisms in place helps. Noh and Kaspar (2003) showed that for those people that experienced racial discrimination, problem-focused social support had reduced levels of depression. Many employers provide counselling services, health and well-being programmes and establish special LGBT (Lesbian, Gay, Bi-sexual or Trans-gender) or women's networks to provide support and work with employers to break down barriers. Though the law provides for a number of protected characteristics it is interesting that these networks are generally not established for people from all protected characteristics groups. This may be as a result of:

- group identity: it may be that an employee has a strong identity with other gay or lesbian people but not as much in common with people of a similar age but different background;

- minority issues: as a minority in the workplace it may be that there are too few employees to establish a group.

Employers need to spend time providing support for those experiencing discrimination but also focus on preventing discrimination. By providing support employers do not condone discrimination but recognize the challenges that employees from minority groups may experience. This ensures that the employer shows that employees are valued for who they are and supported in the work environment. Anti-discrimination rights for a range of protected characteristics can be found through the Equality Act 2010 (before this discrimination legislation was diverse and this Act harmonized discrimination law).

In practice we will find ourselves responsible for anti-discrimination measures, and may negotiate for counselling services as part of the benefits offered by the company. We may also find that we are working with our occupational health provider to offer a well-being programme or with a health and safety officer to tackle risks of work-based stress. In turn this will support our work to reduce grievances and build a positive environment for work. Discrimination is covered in particular in Chapters 4 and 7.

Contractual rights

These are rights that are formed within the employment contract. (It could be argued that work–life balance rights may be expressed within particular contracts, and therefore described as contractual rights, but these have been dealt with separately.)

Implied rights (duties of employer)

There are implied rights (or duties of the employer) which are not stated within the contract but assumed as general duties that all employers have. These include the right to:

- available work and pay;
- respect;
- a suitable and safe working environment;
- a duty of care provided by: competent colleagues, adequate material, proper systems and supervision; and protection against psychiatric harm;
- prompt and proper management of a grievance.

These rights (or employer duties) protect the employment relationship, firstly by providing a protection to the transaction made by the contract – to provide work for pay. The relationship between the two parties is at risk if either work or pay is not provided. Despite the fact that payment for availability may be acceptable to employees, in certain cases the need for work to retain skills and reputation remains. This has been interestingly covered in the case of *William Hill Ltd v Tucker* [1999] ICR 291, where an issue of six-month 'garden leave' was viewed as not acceptable as the employer has an implied right to give the claimant work during the period. It is important to note that the employee had a one-month notice period and the employer was applying for an injunction preventing the claimant from working. It is clear that employees will need protection so that they can continue to work to retain skills and, a clearly fundamental requirement, that they require payment for work completed.

There is a need for mutual respect to maintain the trust and confidence the employee has in the employment relationship. Similarly the employee will need to maintain loyalty and faithfulness to the employer. If the behaviour of the employer (usually the manager) fundamentally breaches the trust and confidence of the employment contract and the employer (manager) treats the employee with such disrespect that it is viewed that the company wishes the employment contract to end, then this may be taken as a dismissal by the employee. This is constructive dismissal which is covered in *HR Fundamentals: Employee Relations* (Aylott, 2014).

An employee has the right to a safe working environment and the employer has a duty of care to provide a working environment in which the employee can carry out their duties. The employee needs to be able to complete work with the resources, systems and supervision available to meet their contractual requirements. Without this the employee could be at risk, either physically or psychologically, or/and will be unable to meet their contractual requirements. Though this right has broad implications, the protection of the employee has associated benefits to the employer, who also wants the work completed.

Finally in *W A Goold (Pearmak) and McConnell* [1995] IRLR 516, the duty of an employer to deal with a grievance properly and promptly was upheld and linked clearly to s.3, Employment Rights Act 1996, where an employee should be given information about the procedure for making a grievance. This implied duty for an employer to comply is fundamental to the employment relationship and, if breached, an employee can resign and claim unfair dismissal (constructive dismissal).

These rights protect employees and enable them to maintain skills, to manage their living expenses with an expected regular income and to carry out their duties, safely, with the resources they need, within an environment of mutual respect, trust and confidence in the relationship.

Express rights

These are rights that have been clearly agreed to and are usually written into the employment contract, one example being the right to notice. This has statutory foundation in s.86, Employment Rights Act (1996). Both parties are subject to notice periods, but when referring to protecting the employee there are minimum periods of notice to be given if the employee is to be dismissed, from one week to 12 weeks dependent on length of service. The employer will have wrongfully dismissed the employee if this notice period or payment in lieu of notice is not given. The employee will be able to claim the lost notice pay through an Employment Tribunal. Notice periods vary in length and are dependent on length or service and seniority.

This right to a notice period is not expected to equate to the actual period it takes an employee to find new employment. This will vary with the economic environment, supply and demand for employment in general and demand for the specific skills that the employee possesses. However, the employee has greater protection if they have not been in the job market for a long time or the type of job that they may be seeking is senior and therefore more difficult to find. Senior employees tend to have a longer notice period.

Dismissal rights

Section 98 of the Employment Rights Act, (1996) provides for fair dismissal from employment, enabling employers to dismiss for:

- capability or qualification, s.2 (a);
- conduct, s.2 (b);
- redundancy, s.2 (c).

It is also possible for an employee to be dismissed if there is a statutory restriction to employment in that position (s.2 (d)): for example, if an employee employed as a driver has been disqualified and there is no alternative work for them. The final fair reason listed in s.98 is some other substantial reason (SOSR) – s.2 (e) – which can be used to justify dismissal to a Tribunal but is rarely relevant to an HR professional in the workplace.

The employee requires protection from unfair dismissal – procedures to ensure that an employee has a thorough investigation, that there is a genuine reason and reasonable grounds for the dismissal. According to the Trade Union Congress (2011) changing employment protection for unfair dismissal from one year to two years affected 3 million employees. This means that employees gain the ability to claim unfair dismissal after two years' service and that before then an employer does not need to follow procedures that would need to be followed after two years. Though the employee is protected against some unfair dismissal at day one of employment (for example, discrimination) the employer is able to easily dismiss an employee before two years, so long as the required notice period is given.

However if an employee has not been able to do the job or reach acceptable standards then it is reasonable for the employer to provide training before dismissing the employee for incapability. If the employee is sick, and unable to do the job because they are on sick leave, it is reasonable for the employer to determine how long the employee will take to get better and equate that with the business needs, acting sympathetically but following procedure if the employee is unable to return to work in reasonable time. Both these procedures (and protections) are only available after two years' service. For misconduct an employee can be dismissed without two years' service without following procedure, which would have provided an opportunity for:

- some investigation of the allegations;
- an ability for the employee to state their case;
- any witnesses to give their accounts;
- time to be taken for a decision to be made.

Unfair dismissal is covered in greater detail in *HR Fundamentals: Employee Relations* (Aylott, 2014).

When it comes to redundancy, employees are only provided with redundancy pay after two years' service. This takes account of the age of the employee and length of service, and therefore can be argued to 'compensate' for any difficulty the employee may have finding new employment. In many ways, in a redundancy situation, employees need time to come to terms with the loss of employment, for the end of the employment relationship, for separation from colleagues and for loss of security. They also need time to prepare for the challenge of seeking new employment. Though in a smaller-scale redundancy this time is not available, for larger-scale redundancy there is time for consultation and time off to find work, both supportive measures that protect the employee.

Automatically unfair dismissal

This is where the more important protections for employees can be found and these are included in the Employment Rights Act 1996 (see Table 2.4).

TABLE 2.4   Unfair dismissal rights in the *Employment Rights Act* 1996

Dismissal for:	Employment Rights Act 1996
being summoned for jury service	s.98(b)
for taking leave for family reasons	s.99
in health and safety cases	s.100
for refusing Sunday working (retail and betting only)	s.101
for working as a trustee of occupational pension schemes	s.102
for being an employee representative (TU representative)	s.103
for making a protected disclosure	s.103(a)
for making an assertion of a statutory right	s.104
for national minimum wage cases	s.104(a)
for tax credit cases	s.104(b)
for requesting flexible working	s.104(c)

Other rights include:

- dismissal for acting as a companion in a dismissal or grievance – s.12, Employment Relations Act 1999 (the right to be accompanied is found in ss. 10–15, Employment Relations Act 1999 as amended by the Employment Relations Act 2004);

- dismissal for reason of age, disability, gender reassignment, marriage and civil partnership, race, religion or belief, sex and sexual orientation, pregnancy and maternity: this would be viewed as direct discrimination, s.13, Equality Act 2010.

All these rights protect the employee in order, for example, that they can play their part in society, request their legal rights without fear of dismissal, and inform the correct authorities about wrong-doing within an organization without fear (if the correct procedures are followed) and to protect other employees from health and safety risks. These rights mean that employees cannot be dismissed for carrying out any of these actions, but it does not mean that employees can run amok accusing employers of wrong-doing. For example, according to the Public Interest Disclosure Act 1998 that covers whistle-blowing (making a protected disclosure), the whistle-blower:

- must have a genuine belief in the information being disclosed;
- must not do this to make personal gain;
- must show it is reasonable to make the disclosure;
- must disclose information to a prescribed person.

Protecting employers

Employers are subject to a range of legislation, of which employment law is just one part. Businesses need to obtain and manage their credit, protect investors, often need to trade across borders, and must meet their tax liabilities; the employment of workers is one small area of their activity which is subject to legislation. The World Bank (2012) has assessed that the UK is seventh in world ranking and the USA is fourth when it comes to the ease with which an employer may do business (the impact of regulation on business). The UK in particular has been working to reduce the burden of regulation on business, in order to encourage business innovation and growth, with a review of existing regulation and assessment of the impact of new regulation (Department for Business, Innovation and Skills, 2012). This review of regulation also includes employment law, both domestic and European.

Despite the argument that protection for the employee, the weaker party in the employment relationship, is provided by the State, the 'third force' in this relationship (Poole, 1980), employment law also has some benefit for employers. It provides a framework in which employers are able to follow best practice, enabling them to be competitive. Much of the law supports companies to work effectively and to improve their relations with employees, to get the best out of them. In fact evidence from the World Bank shows that whilst the USA is fourth regarding the ease of doing business and it is easiest in the USA to make employees redundant, it continues to struggle economically (Davis, 2011), so reducing regulation is not the panacea to all ills.

It is clear that relaxing regulation does not lead solely to more competitive and successful companies and the argument is aptly put by the World Bank (2011: 93) '*smart employment regulation, which enhances job security and improves productivity through employer-worker cooperation, means that both workers and firms benefit*'. However many smaller employers are ignorant of or avoid the law and though the UK is attempting to improve its record, the monitoring, support and enforcement of employment law has been poor (Pollert, 2007). This puts small employers at risk of costly Employment Tribunal cases, which if lost may impact on their future and that of their employees.

The role of legislation in supporting employers

Employment law will protect and support employers to improve their employee relations and gain competitive advantage. The three following legal examples support this.

The beginning of the employment relationship – written statement of particulars

Whilst there is no legislation that enforces an induction process, employers are required by law to provide a written statement which provides the basics of the contract and the job description, Employment Rights Act 1996, s.1. This is common sense – an employee needs to quickly recognize what is required so that they can become effective. The cost of recruiting and selecting employees (advertising and agency fees) now stands at £2,000 for the average employee and £5,000 for senior management (Chartered Institute of Personnel and Development, 2013b) and this does not account for any of the additional costs of recruitment (for example, induction training, lost productivity). Any loss of an employee over the first year means another unnecessary and costly recruitment process that we as HR professionals have to carry out. In fact the induction crisis, when an employee questions their decision to join the company and assesses whether it was flawed, can be prompted by small factors but it is the cumulative experience of joining the company that can help an employee decide whether to remain or resign (Pilbream and Corbridge, 2010). Factors such as a written contract and job description can play their part.

Usually large employers have employment contracts and it is the smaller employer that is more vulnerable here. In fact smaller employers (250 employees or less) tend to have more Employment Tribunal claims and are more likely to lose a claim (Saridakis *et al*, 2008). It is only when a claim is lost that the lack of a written statement or contract will be relevant, and the employer made to pay for their neglect.

During the employment relationship – discrimination

The Equality Act 2010 harmonized discrimination legislation, but for many employers the law remains complex. The lack of a cap on compensation payments and the ability to claim for injury of feelings makes it difficult for any employer to welcome this legislation.

When we look at diversity it is more than meeting legal requirements for equal opportunities but how harnessing differences will support the business. According to Mullins (2010) the reasons for the focus on diversity have been numerous. There are demographic changes in the workforce beyond the increasing number of part-time workers and women that have joined the workforce in the past few years. Along with changes in the UK's workforce demographics there has been change in the demographics of the customer base, extending at times beyond the UK with the globalization of the marketplace. Existing social attitudes towards diversity have changed in the UK, as has legislation, both of which encourage an ongoing change in social attitudes. Finally, as the Leitch Report (2006) described, there is a shortage of higher level skills, which impacts, according to Leitch, on the ability of the UK to reap the full benefits of new technology and to develop industry.

Acas (2012a) believes that there is *'clear competitive advantage to be gained by employing a diverse workforce'* and this is expanded by the Chartered Institute of Personnel and Development (2012d) to be viewed as three strands:

- people issues;
- competitiveness;
- market reputation.

We need to recruit, train and promote the best employees using the talent within the organization regardless of any irrelevant differences between individuals. Excluding any particular group has no sound business sense; it eliminates a potential source of talent and, particularly where this is a rare skill, it prevents the organization from reaching its full competitive advantage. Once a diverse workforce is working together, research has shown that a diverse team is more creative (Collett, 1999). This supports the employer's ability to be competitive, to solve problems and meet the needs of a diverse customer base. With customers and investors increasingly interested in corporate social responsibility, a diverse workforce can support the reputation of the employer's brand.

Despite the arguments made by Acas (2012a) and the Chartered Institute of Personnel and Development (2012d), assumptions must be challenged and evidence reviewed concerning the business case for diversity. It is difficult to find evidence, other than business case studies, which reinforce the assertions made by those proposing a business case and in fact Esmail *et al* (2005) do not find enough evidence to support diversity on the business case alone. Mullins (2010) recognizes that increasing diversity may lead to reduced harmony as there is less cultural commonality to help team cohesion. So the business case alone may not be enough to encourage employers to fully welcome a diverse workforce; it is the social justice argument, the need for businesses to meet the change in attitudes and be seen to do the right thing, that should encourage employers to embrace diversity.

CASE STUDY   Diversity

The effect that diversity and diversity policies have had on business is best illustrated by the case studies produced by the Chartered Institute of Personnel and Development (2005) and the Confederation of British Industry (2008), and two examples of real practice are given here.

HSBC is one of the largest banking and financial institutions in the world, with its headquarters in London but offices in over 80 different countries (HSBC, 2013a). Their view on diversity is as follows:

We believe that diversity brings only benefits for our customers, our business and our people. The more different perspectives we have, the better equipped we'll be to meet the demands of our hugely diverse global customer base (HSBC, 2013b).

Hilary Wiseman, Head of Diversity in the UK and Europe explains how their approach to diversity has supported HSBC:

We have the benefit of working within a global organization with an extremely diverse workforce. In 2004 we had 10,000 branches and offices located in 76 countries and territories. Of our 69,000 managers globally in 2004, only 30 per cent were white and male. We have a huge diversity of problem-solving capabilities and thinking styles to choose from. We know that, if we don't employ a diverse workforce in Birmingham, for instance, we won't be as successful in attracting new customers. That's why over 49 per cent of recruits in that area were from ethnic minorities during 2004. We know that if we hadn't employed a Chinese speaker on the counter at Coventry, we wouldn't have attracted an extra half a million pounds' worth of business within six months of a single conversation. We know that if we hadn't learned about the impact of Sharia law from our own people, we wouldn't have been able to launch HSBC Amanah Finance, which enables Muslims in the UK to own their own homes. This is a service which is now envied by many other UK Financial Services companies and is world-renowned for being one of the most important, impactful and successful product launches we have ever celebrated (Chartered Institute of Personnel and Development, 2005: 20).

Intercontinental Hotels Group has nine hotel brands including Holiday Inn, Crowne Plaza Hotels and Intercontinental Hotels. They took an innovative approach to changes in disability legislation by targeting disabled people as potential recruits. In 2006, their recruitment day resulted in four disabled candidates being offered jobs, and 12 more participating in a training programme which led to a further four being offered a job and after a work placement one other disabled candidate gaining a role. Intercontinental Hotels Group have only had to make minor adjustments to help these candidates fulfil their roles and are convinced that the programme has helped them gain a new pool of talent, develop line managers, support teamwork and reduce absence and turnover. According to the Confederation of British Industry (2008: 20):

Ultimately, it has demonstrated IHG's commitment to recognising employees as individuals and for what they can bring to the business, which every employee can appreciate – not just those with disabilities.

The end of the employment relationship – fair dismissal

Unfair dismissal is a relatively new concept, coming into being with the Industrial Relations Act 1971 and so it could be argued that there is little need to provide protection or support for businesses. If they could dismiss as they wished without sanction, to some extent the current situation for employees with less than two years' service, then it would give employers the flexibility they need. But it is the process that must be followed that is all important (and this process is covered in more detail in *HR Fundamentals: Employee Relations* (Aylott, 2014)). Examples of issues that we may come across and that may require the use of the discipline procedure are lateness, unauthorized absence, insubordination or fraud. Lateness and unauthorized absence can be resolved without the need for dismissal and enable the employer to keep employees focused on their work performance, but insubordination and fraud are serious and may result in dismissal.

Though the Employment Rights Act 1996, s.98 gives reasons for fair dismissal, it is case law that provides guidance for Employment Tribunals. In *Iceland Frozen Foods v Jones* (1983) ICR 17, Mr Justice Browne-Wilkinson gave a five-step approach for Tribunals to determine whether the action has been reasonable. This included looking at the '*band of reasonable responses... within which one employer might reasonably take one view, another quite reasonably take another*'. This means that an employer is tested on their reasonableness, not what an Employment Tribunal expects as best practice.

We might be forgiven for assuming that a test of reasonableness is quite broad. If employees believe that their employer will act (and has proved to act) unreasonably, then they feel their jobs may be at risk. There is no procedural or informational justice and whether there is distributive justice, whether the outcome is fair to the employee, is seen as the arbitrary decision of management and not a logical one. This uncertainty and lack of trust does not build an atmosphere conducive to efficient and effective productivity; it builds an atmosphere of fear, with high absence and turnover.

However if we have:

- provided a transparent formal process for the management of misconduct and capability issues;
- investigated all discipline issues thoroughly; and

- used that investigation to formulate a genuine belief on reasonable grounds,

then we may be seen to have met the 'Burchell test' based on *British Homes Stores v Burchell* (1980) ICR 303. An employer who takes this approach will have the reputation of being a fair employer, and though at times may make the wrong decision, and cause the dismissal of an employee that has not erred, the fact that they have investigated thoroughly and made their decision on reasonable grounds and acting 'within the bands of reasonable responses' will mean that they are still viewed as a reasonable employer. Their reputation will encourage new recruits to apply and retain existing trained employees.

Keeping up to date

It is important that we keep up to date with employment law changes. In the UK, statutes are usually introduced twice a year, often in the spring and autumn. This means that HR professionals can be prepared for any major changes, and can follow the process of any Bill through Parliament, to anticipate any relevant actions they and their employer will need to take. For example, the Enterprise and Regulatory Reform HC Bill (2012–13) (7) was presented to Parliament in May 2012, gained Royal Assent in April 2013, and became statute, the Enterprise and Regulatory Reform Act 2013. Whilst it was going through Parliament, we as HR professionals will have been aware of the impact of the proposed law in terms of settlement agreements and unfair dismissal for political opinions. By the time it gained Royal Assent the content of the law had been regularly in the public domain, and in particular discussed by the Chartered Institute of Personnel and Development. Most HR professionals would have not come to it unprepared.

When it comes to case law we also need to keep up to date. Statutes provide main points and general principles but case law will interpret this. Judges give guidance by means of their judgment which can guide HR professionals in their development of policy and procedure, in their advice to line managers or in their work directly with employees. Many of the concerns that line managers have about employment law comes from their understandable ignorance of employment law or their knowledge of law gained through the media.

How to keep up to date

Not all employers have the financial capacity to have access to up-to-date legal references. Some overcome this by taking legal advice when dealing with difficult employee cases, but many require the HR professional to have the up-to-date knowledge of changes to employment law and practice.

As a member of the Chartered Institute of Personnel and Development we can access *Employment Law at Work*, which includes changes to legislation and case reports and practical application of law in, for example, factsheets and podcasts. The Chartered Institute of Personnel and Development also provides access to journals, but care should be taken to ensure that these relate to the country that the HR professional is practising in.

Advice and guidance on applying employment law can be accessed at the Acas website, and following the relevant Code of Practice will support us to protect employers against Employment Tribunal cases. Gov.UK, which replaces Business Link and Directgov internet sources, provides a simple guide to employment law and employment rights and is more relevant to direct employees to if they want impartial and free information. Many, but not all of the other free online sources are supplied by legal firms. Some provide free and relevant statute and case law, such as employmentcasesupdate.co.uk and others provide some basic information but advertise further advice for payment. Other online sites such as XpertHR provide extensive and up-to-date case law and other advice but require a subscription, or are solely employment law sources such as Westlaw.

Conclusion

We have seen that employment law provides protection for the weaker party, enables society to function, and employees to provide for their families without exploitation and with limited insecurity. However this should not be at the expense of business, which needs to be successful for the economic future of the country. Our quality of life, our ability to find employment and build a life depends on the success of our businesses, and these cannot be obstructed by law. Employment law needs to work for both parties.

In the next chapter we will examine the effect employment law has on business and HR strategy. We will review the changing legal and moral framework for employers and the issues and challenges that occur at different stages in the business lifecycle. But to finish this chapter we take a look at the value of whistle-blowing.

CASE STUDY   Whistle-blowing

It is difficult for an employee to expose wrong-doings or malpractice. Examples abound of when employees have failed to raise an issue or issues have not been acted upon. These include the Clapham Junction Rail Crash 1988, where 35 passengers and crew died. Here the Hidden Enquiry identified that during an alteration to the signalling, poor practice led to a wire remaining in contact with its old circuit and able to feed into the new circuit. This should have been noted by a wire count, which was not carried out by the workman, supervisor or tester, despite records being signed to confirm that the test had been completed. The engineering works team had worked together for many years, and was supervised by Mr Lippett, an outsider. He had seen the poor workmanship, but not mentioned it to management because he did not want to '*rock the boat*' (Hidden, 1989: 97).

It is usually one person who is in the position of being there at the right time to identify malpractice, but it is difficult for that person to speak out. The following example shows the difference that can be made, both to the organization, in this case the NHS, to colleagues and to customers, in this case patients.

Nick Harper was a consultant anaesthetist, fairly new in his role. He worked with one surgeon, whose patients regularly lost more blood than the others and there were a number of patients that gave Nick particular concern. It was very early on in his role with the NHS Trust, when working with this surgeon, one patient died. Nick Harper felt this was an unnecessary death but when discussing it with the surgeon his lack of experience meant that nothing came of the discussion. Nick Harper decided that he would make regular records when he worked with this surgeon. After 12 months there was another difficult case and Nick then felt he could not continue to work with the surgeon and he took his concerns to the Senior Medical Council. Following this there was an investigation and the surgeon was suspended. The result of the process was that the surgeon was removed by the General Medical Council and he was also convicted of manslaughter.

Nick Harper found it very difficult to make this disclosure, particularly as he was a new member of the team and the surgeon was a longstanding employee. Many colleagues kept Nick at a distance. According to Syedain (2012) he also experienced a member of staff pouring a pint of beer over him, and it is clear that despite the fact that colleagues in the Anaesthetic Department also had the same experience with the surgeon, it was very difficult for Nick Harper to voice these concerns formally (Syedain, 2012; The *Guardian*, 2011).

In both these cases it can be seen that by identifying and communicating malpractice, following a legal process, would have protected the employer. In one case the employer was eventually protected, despite the loss of at least one patient's life; in the other case the employee felt unable to speak and protect the employer, and 35 passengers and rail employees died.

Employment law and strategy

03

INTRODUCTION

We as HR professionals are bound by the Code of Professional Conduct (Chartered Institute of Personnel and Development, 2012c) to advise management within the law. Our advice is not always followed and at times meeting legal requirements may cost the business more than not meeting them. Managers may balance the risk of Employment Tribunal and reputation against doing something that is illegal but take a view that the action is unlikely to have a major adverse impact on the business. However, we must follow our Code of Conduct, be mindful of the needs of both employer and employee and cannot advise an employer to act illegally. This chapter discusses the dilemmas that meeting legislative demands can produce. It also discusses the link between business strategy and lifecycle and the focus of employment law.

In this chapter we will explore:

- the changing legal and moral framework for employers;
- the difference between transactional and transformational leadership with reference to values and law;
- approaches to business strategy and compliance with the law;
- the issues and challenges that occur at different stages in the business lifecycle.

A legal and moral framework

Over time the law has evolved to reflect what is and is not acceptable to society. For example, in the past in the UK child labour was cheap and accepted by the masses as a method of reducing their poverty and providing apprenticeship training. In fact in 1818, 4.5 per cent of the cotton factory labour force consisted of under 10 year olds and 21.5 per cent were under 13 (Freudenberger *et al*, 1984). The Factory Act 1819 restricted child labour to 16 hours per day for all children under 16 years of age (Parliament UK, 2013). This was to be implemented by magistrates, many of whom turned a blind eye to the legislation and did not enforce the Act. Now in the UK the youngest age a child can take up any part-time work is at 13 (Gov.UK, 2013b) and this is restricted to a maximum of 12 hours per week during term-time and 25 hours per week during school holidays (Gov.UK, 2013d). So we can see how our views of child labour have altered.

In the same year, 1819, 11 people were killed and many people were injured in the Peterloo Massacre – they were marching to seek Parliamentary reform, for wider voting rights and trade unionism (BBC, 2008) aspects of life taken for granted in the UK today. Now we in the UK have universal suffrage, the vote from age 18 – and there is even some pressure to reduce the voting age to 16 – and Trade Union membership is no longer illegal. Again, the value of universal voting rights and the right to a collective voice have changed, and in fact the International Labour Organization views the right of association (as a Trade Union) as a basic right.

The legal and moral framework for employers and stakeholders

Employers, particularly small or medium-sized enterprises or SMEs – those businesses with less than 250 employees – are concerned about the amount of bureaucratic legislation with which a business must comply. Employers are bound by more than employment legislation; they also have to comply with company and business legislation. This restricts an employer's ability to compete globally against countries where legislative regulation is more lax, despite the role of the International Labour Organization in attempting to provide a standard playing field (International Labour Organization, 2013b). Domestic law is driven in part by the values and concerns of society, which may mean that certain legislation is gold-plated (Confederation of British Industry, 2010), for example the implementation of European Union legislation by UK domestic law which the Confederation of British Industry has argued extends further than the European Union requires, putting an undue burden on business.

Those of us that work in SMEs will have experienced the burden of legislation and may be aware of the resentment of managers attempting to do business within the legislative boundaries, particularly if their competitors work under less stringent laws. The impact of Employment Tribunal costs can be relatively high for SMEs.

Larger employers have a concern about their reputation and brand image and have to comply with legislation to maintain their good name. Organizations such as M&S need to ensure that their people management policies are clear and available to both employees and investors (M&S, 2013). HR professionals working for larger employers will have established policies and procedures. Larger employers may have a team of HR specialists, a central shared service where line managers and employees can seek advice on policies (as well as managing routine HR tasks) and Business Partners who will work with middle and senior managers implementing policy and supporting more strategic business decisions with advice.

Both large and small employers are equally constrained by a common set of values which are reflected in law. Employers competing effectively and exporting produce enable the country to bring in external funds to support the economy, and eventually the quality of life of its nationals. However if this is at the expense of national values, if for example, it is achieved with the use of child labour, for many this would not be acceptable. We have a legal and moral framework within which we judge our decisions.

If we do not keep to this framework there are some implications for all involved professionals. For example, directors have general duties under the Company Act 2006. They must act in the best interests of their company and promote its success. Whilst there is no general duty to act within the law, it can be argued that by acting illegally a director may not be working for the success of the company, by damaging its good name. The consequences of a breach may be minimal – the director may be personally liable for compensation or the company may take legal action for an injunction to prevent the illegal action being taken. However, if it is an issue of discrimination then a director may be personally taken to an Employment Tribunal and their career could be damaged.

For HR professionals the Code of Professional Conduct states that Chartered Institute of Personnel and Development members should '*exhibit and defend professional and personal integrity and honesty at all times*' and '*challenge others if they suspect unlawful or unethical conduct or behaviour*' (Chartered Institute of Personnel and Development, 2012f: 2). Whilst the Chartered Institute of Personnel and Development have the power to revoke an HR professional's Chartered Institute of Personnel and Development membership, this unfortunately does not preclude them from practising as an HR professional in those positions that do not ask for membership. This means that they may still be able to practise but only in a more junior role, as increasingly employers are recognizing the value of Chartered Institute of Personnel and Development membership as a measure of a professional's knowledge and experience.

The law, ethics and organizational values

Organizations have values which are agreed and communicated and against which policies may be measured. Those employees that are part of the organization are expected by HR to have similar values to the organization. This is known as an unitarist approach. In a pluralist organization dissention is expected and it is accepted that not all employees:

- have the same values as the organization;
- have the best interests of the employer at heart;
- agree with the approach that the employer has chosen.

However it is expected that the employee carries out their job and meets their obligations to the employer, regardless of their own values. If they are part of the organization they might not have the same values as the organization but they should at least comply with the organization and in all aspects of their work represent the organization as if they did have the same values.

Certain values may not initially appear to breach employment law but we may have a problem if we were to base our decisions not on the law but on corporate values. For example employers that work in a highly pressurized environment, that promote risk-taking, speed, action and results are likely to find corners are cut, as the following case study shows.

CASE STUDY   Valuing risk-taking – a cautionary tale

The cause of the recession of 2008 and the economic crisis that ensued is complex but the extent of risk-taking in the banking sector was a critical factor. In the USA sub-prime mortgages relied on house prices increasing for the debt to be paid – but when house prices fell there were inevitable defaults on these loans. The mortgage-backed securities market (in which it is particularly difficult to value or determine the risk of assets), felt the impact of these defaults, and as the packaged debts had been spread globally, the losses were also spread globally. Well-renowned financial organizations began to struggle as the extent of the losses or confidence in their security fell. In the USA, Lehman Brothers was declared bankrupt, Merrill Lynch was bought by Bank of America and in the UK Northern Rock was bailed out by the Government, HBOS was bought by Lloyds TSB, Bradford and Bingley was nationalized and Lloyds TSB and RBS partially nationalized. Some of this impact was from the sale of mortgages but banks such as RBS had been particularly active in the sub-prime market.

The circumstances that encouraged banks such as the RBS to take these risks have been researched by the University of Leicester (Kerr and Robinson, 2012). They suggest that the management practices, including threats of redundancy, alongside aggressive sales targets, together with the pressure for status both internally and amongst other banks led to the bank's decline. For the Government and financial regulators the cause includes the remuneration packages of senior managers.

The House of Commons Treasury Committee (2009: 5) *'found that bonus-driven remuneration structures encouraged reckless and excessive risk-taking and that the design of bonus schemes was not aligned with the interests of shareholders and the long-term sustainability of the banks'*, and the Financial Services Authority stated that *'we consider that inappropriate remuneration policies were a contributory factor behind the market crisis. We introduced the Code because we found that fundamental changes in the approach many firms adopted to remuneration were needed to ensure we have a solid foundation to avoid future crises'*. The Financial Services Authority Code of Practice for remuneration in the financial sector (Financial Services Authority, 2011) attempted to prevent high bonus pay-outs encouraging employees to carry out high-risk activities for short-term gain. The code stipulated that bonus payments should be paid out over longer periods to ensure a longer term view.

For the HR professional it is important to understand the values of the organization, and how they are interpreted through its policies and procedures. We need to ensure that they work towards the long-term benefit of the company and that any actions encouraged by these values are both legal and ethical.

We can better understand the way in which the organization's values are communicated when we examine the type of leadership used in the business. Some leaders are transactional, rewarding employees for effort but not going further than legal obligations. The transformational leader (Burns, 1978) always returns to the needs and wants of their followers and possesses a moral higher purpose. The transformational leader wishes to engage in the motives of the followers. Though Bass (1985) does not emphasize the moral imperative as Burns does, it is clear that influencing others using inspirational motivation is important. The transformational leader 'transforms' the team by influencing them, meeting their needs and wants and inspiring them with a higher purpose, beyond their own. The transformational leader as employer does this by using the values and mission of the organization to inspire them, at times deciding to do more than the law requires – for example providing a better redundancy package than the statutory requirement.

Whether the leaders of an organization use transactional or transformational leaders or have a unitarist or pluralist approach, the organization does have its own values. These are communicated through the organization and all policies and procedures are aligned to them. Most organizational values and the approaches that they purport to take in practice tend to follow legislation and a transactionalist leadership approach rarely goes further than legal requirements. A transformational leader will make decisions based on the values and vision of the organization, and may well not always choose the easier path, but may go beyond legal compliance to support their team, treat them better than the law requires.

The role of the HR professional

Our role is to provide legal advice and support in terms of policies and procedures that can protect the employer and employee and enable the company to get the best out of its employees and improve the company's performance. To do this effectively it is helpful if we have an understanding of the factors involved in driving the business strategy and the stages of the organization's lifecycle.

Business strategy and legal compliance

The business strategy may be to compete on innovation, cost reduction or quality enhancement (Porter, 1985). That is to lead on price, offering cheap products or services, or lead on differentiation, selling products or services with different features or benefits to the customer but with a higher price, either based on innovation or quality enhancement.

Whilst it is easy to state that each business strategy merely needs to meet legal requirements, it may be that the challenges are different. Employers that offer cheaper products or services will have to cut costs as much as possible to be competitive with others in the market. The challenge that they face is to cut costs but not to an extent that the employer cannot provide full training or does not meet health and safety obligations or other legal requirements. If an employer makes cuts too acutely then it risks additional unplanned costs from either Employment Tribunals or a claim of negligence through the civil, and for health and safety omissions through the criminal, court system. If the business strategy is differentiation then the employer still needs to ensure that legal requirements are fully met but this is less of a risk.

Lifecycle – small and medium-sized enterprises

HR strategy and practices differ depending on the stage of 'life' an organization has reached (Kochan and Barocci, 1985). When an organization is small, HR practices are informal. For example, small businesses tend to use local advertisements and personal recommendations (Vinten, 1998) and increasingly have a Web presence. These practices are informal and unstructured. It is unlikely that there is any HR provision and often it is the owner of the business that carries out any HR responsibilities. SMEs lack the resources to keep up to date with legislative changes and so can be vulnerable in this regard. In fact there is a correlation between the size of organization and unfair dismissal claims, with smaller organizations having the bulk of claims against them. This could be due to a lack of knowledge and formal procedures in SMEs but may also be attributed to more volatile or personal responses to dismissal in a smaller firm. Whatever, the fact remains that over three-fifths of claims are made against businesses with fewer than 50 employees (Tremlett and Banerji, 1994).

Some small organizations seek advice or may occasionally outsource their HR responsibilities. In the UK, small businesses may seek the assistance of consultants who may, for example, help them write an employee handbook or policies, or may advise on particular discipline or grievance issues. Generally SMEs tend to keep the operational HR in-house and to outsource areas of their HR strategy to consultants (Chartered Institute of Personnel and Development, 2013a). In the USA, SMEs outsource to a professional employer organization that effectively employs workers for the SME (Klaas, 2003).

Small businesses in the UK can obtain advice from the Federation of Small Businesses which not only provides advice but will also offer legal insurance. This is similar to other legal insurance schemes, so that if the small business has taken the advice given they can have both legal representation and some coverage for basic awards and any compensation awarded if they lose the case. Sources such as smallbusiness.co.uk (run by a media company as an online magazine) can provide advice for small businesses, and others such as the Citizens Advice Bureau or Acas can provide information on legal issues.

SMEs have to evaluate the cost of consultancy advice or legal insurance against the risk to the business of an Employment Tribunal. Of course any insurance has restrictions which need to be met to trigger the payment, and legal insurance is no exception. Many small business employers avoid thinking about employment law issues, and focus on building their business. In fact they lay themselves open to claims when they could have thought ahead and protected their business.

Lifecycles – growth and maturity

As an organization grows and matures it should develop formal processes and procedures that protect it. The need for specialists becomes more apparent, mainly the need for a professional HR department, even if this consists of just one or two HR generalists. Then as the business grows the HR department will begin to specialize, with possibly compensation and benefits specialists or employee relation specialists. Alternatively, as the business grows, the organization may choose to structure the HR department with three key elements (Ulrich and Brockbank, 2008):

- a shared services centre which will provide operational support for line managers and employees, managing repetitive administrative processes and providing both line managers and employees with guidance on company procedures;

- business partners who work closely with line managers or senior managers to support and implement business strategy with the guidance of HR;

- centres of excellence – teams of specialists able to manage complex problems with innovative approaches (Chartered Institute of Personnel and Development, 2012e).

All three elements of the HR professional structure described above will have to refer to legislation. The shared service centre will at the very least deal with transactional issues but there is a trend for transformational issues, such as providing more detailed advice regarding call-centre technology (Arkin, 1999). Shared services centres may also be responsible for global as well as national regions and so will need to have access to procedures and legislation for those areas using the shared service centre. Business partners will refer to practical issues, supporting line managers to implement strategy, and to plan and develop talent and to manage and implement change – and the implications of employment law on all of these. Employee relations and employment law specialists support line managers to manage complex employee relations issues which may not have been managed effectively or may have the potential of becoming Employment Tribunal cases.

Lifecycles – decline

If an organization is in decline then the HR focus is one of rationalization, restructure and redundancy. As employers reduce the number of trained and experienced employees they reduce the potential for the organization to flexibly meet new demands. Employers have to balance the need to cut costs with the need to retain talent, and at some point the redundancies will impact on the employer's ability to do business. We as HR professionals in declining businesses will need a good understanding of legislation surrounding redundancy in order to protect the employer from Employment Tribunal claims.

Though the extent of our expertise tends to stop at insolvency, an understanding of this may be helpful to us as we support employees in this situation. When a business becomes unprofitable, it may go into administration or liquidation. If the business goes into administration it means that an attempt to rescue it is made, and if the company is sold as a going concern it is probable that employees' jobs may be retained. However if the company goes into liquidation it is wound-up, which means that creditors and others that are owed money by the business are paid out of any sale of assets. In this case the employees will be given a claim form RP1 which they can use to claim their redundancy payment from the Redundancy Payment Office (Department for Business, Innovation and Skills, 2011b).

Advice and guidance

As HR professionals we may need to give line managers advice over complex issues, taking account of the legal implications, the needs of the business, the impact on employees and the performance of the company. At times we will be able to apply our understanding of the law to the situation, particularly if we have had previous experience of a similar situation. A vital skill for the HR professional is recognition of when the issue extends beyond our knowledge and experience. There will be times when seeking legal advice is necessary, and it is more likely to be of help in the earlier stages of a problem. However we also have a wealth of employment law resource available through the Chartered Institute of Personnel and Development and books such as this one. These resources will enable us to keep up to date and manage the majority of issues within the workplace.

Courage to challenge

The HR Professions Map refers to a number of behaviours relevant to the practice of the profession. Of these the courage to challenge is one, along with being a skilled influencer and being personally credible. These three behaviours need to work together if we are to promote ideas that get accepted and to challenge proposals to ensure they meet legal requirements.

The Chartered Institute of Personnel and Development (2012f) describes the courage to challenge as '*shows courage and confidence to speak up skilfully challenging others even when confronted with resistance or unfamiliar circumstances*'. But to achieve this we need to be able to gain commitment and support from others and combine our HR and commercial acumen to appear professionally able. We need to be seen as colleagues with whom senior managers can converse about difficult issues, where honesty and openness is valued and with whom all feel that they are listened to. We should be known for taking a clear stand for the organization, even if this means standing alone on particular issues.

The role of the HR professional in a global business

Employment law can vary fundamentally from country to country but certain groups of countries have some similarity in approach. For example English speaking countries and former British colonies have similar approaches, using a common law adversarial approach, whilst the French, Southern European countries and their former colonies have a codified system, with detailed codes which describe the way the law should be interpreted. Judges then apply these to the cases that are before them. There are also countries that use religious law such as Islamic Sharia law, though this may be interpreted differently in different Islamic countries.

Multinational corporations

The extent of regulation may differ from country to country and this may influence where multinational corporations choose to establish subsidiaries. Though business regulation may be an aspect of the choice, there are other criteria to be taken into account when making an investment of this kind. The business case, including the potential for growth and profit, is a key driver. Studies have shown the following three criteria are important to a business (Sun, 2002):

- political and economic stability;
- the ease of investment – that is the administrative and regulatory process to enable the business to enter and operate in the market;
- the infrastructure including communications, road and rail systems and available labour.

Some businesses may be dissuaded from operating in a country because:

- the entry procedures are too burdensome (eg the need for visas and work permits or the registration of the company);
- procedures governing the site location (eg building regulations) may be too restrictive;
- operating procedures (eg health and safety regulations, employment law or tax reporting legislation) are problematic. (Businesses may be dissuaded if tax rates are particularly high, reducing their available profit if they operated in that country.)

So the choice of country for a subsidiary will be influenced by employment law and regulation but this is just one of the many factors that may persuade a multinational corporation to invest in that country.

Once with a subsidiary, factory or logistics site in the country there are other issues that may influence the approach to law. The company may take an ethnocentric strategic business approach, and HRM transfers the policies and procedures of the headquarters to the subsidiary within the confines of local law. A polycentric strategic business approach may be taken, where the subsidiary is allowed to adopt local practices and so the parent company takes an adaptive approach to HRM policies and procedures. This will mean that they reflect the culture of the country, along with its laws.

Despite the different global approaches to strategy for multinational corporations and their subsidiaries, the fact remains that any central policies and procedures will need to meet with the employment legislation of the country. Within the European Union there is a degree of convergence in employment law. European Union regulations are enforceable in their existing form whilst European Union directives can be interpreted into domestic law, so long as a minimum of the directive is included. This provides a minimum level of similar regulation across Europe. Internationally the International Labour Organization provides a similar role in establishing minimum labour standards worldwide. It produces conventions which if ratified will be binding on the country and so are viewed to some degree as international law.

Conclusion

In this chapter we have realized that society's values change, that basing decisions on company values may be problematic, that the law provides a solid foundation to support decision-making, and that transformational leaders often go beyond mere compliance with the law. We reviewed the views of law and approaches to it of SMEs and larger organizations, and the impact that business strategy and the lifecycle of the company might have on the implementation of employment law. We also examined the role of the HR professional to give advice and challenge decisions whether this is in a SME, domestic company or a multinational corporation. In the next chapter we look at the practical issue of how employment law impacts in the workplace, from the start of the employment relationship to when an employee leaves the business.

In our final case study below we look at changing views of discriminatory practice and how this has informed statute and case law.

CASE STUDY Shifting values

One of the most complex areas of employment law is that of discrimination (covered in Chapters 2, 4 and 7). It is a developing area as society's views have changed. In 1898 it was possible to '*refuse to employ [an individual] for the most mistaken, capricious, malicious or morally reprehensible motives that can be conceived, but [that individual] as no right of action against him*' (*Allen v Flood* (1998) AC1 172–173). The law did not protect against discrimination.

When in 1925 a Labour-run council, Poplar Borough Council, attempted to pay men and women equally, it was viewed as so unreasonable as to be outside their powers as trustees of ratepayers' money (*Roberts v Hopwood* [1925] AC 578, 594). We have seen how society's views have changed radically. In this case, using their Labour values, Poplar Borough Council was seen to go beyond the law and beyond what was acceptable by society at that time. Using our own values we may find that at times we break new ground but it put Poplar Borough Council through a costly court case which was lost. According to Lord Atkinson the council had '*allowed themselves to be guided in preference by some eccentric principles of socialistic philanthropy, or by a feminist ambition to secure the equality of the sexes in the matter of wages in the world of labour*'. The Labour-run council could not rely on their own values as it put the council at risk of a court case with associated costs.

The Poplar incident shows that we cannot rely on our own values at work. Can we rely on corporate values? Now corporate businesses have their own particular image that illustrates their values: for example the image of M&S is of a reliable company producing quality clothes, known as a fair employer. Image is all important as the business environment becomes more and more competitive. The competitive edge is now focused less on the characteristics of the product and more on the image created by the company. Businesses use many subtle ploys to compete. An attractive person may be used in an advertisement or a company may use a woman to lead a bid for a contract not because of her skills but to show the diversity of their staff.

Virgin Rail had a difficult situation with unfortunate female blouses which had caused complaint – unfortunate because these provided the opportunity for an accusation of exploitation. Virgin Rail's female staff had complained that their blouses were 'flimsy and revealing' (The *Telegraph*, 2013) though there was no accusation of exploitation and it was likely to have been a poor design decision rather than a business decision. Virgin Rail quickly worked to resolve the complaint.

The real business decisions that do exploit women or remove people with protected characteristics from front-facing business are more subtle and sometimes far beyond what can be evidenced at Employment Tribunal. However we have a responsibility to protect both the employer and employees, and we can see that these subtle areas put our employers at risk – not only from litigation but also the reputation that will prevent talented people from applying to join our businesses.

We cannot rely on changing society's values or corporate values. We can rely on our own, but only in respect of our own experience. For example, when talking about a course on business ethics, Donna Sockell (2013) relates that '*another young alumna observed and was deeply affected by sexual harassment in a workplace that prided itself on being a values-driven, progressive company. Her parents told her that such experiences were common for women in business and suggested she let it go, but she spoke up and chose to leave a company that tolerated such behaviour*'. We might not wish to take cases to Tribunal ourselves but removing ourselves, and our talent, from such organizations is a way we can influence a company by our own values.

When we look at the HR professional's role to protect the business we cannot rely on own values or that of the company. The actions of the company will be measured against the law and the final arbiter in these matters is the law.

PART TWO

IN PRACTICE

How it works

04

INTRODUCTION

The HR professional applies employment legislation and case law to the routine activities of the workplace to protect employers from costly Employment Tribunal claims. This chapter, and the one that follows it, will be particularly relevant to the practising HR professional. In this chapter we review the influence of employment law in practice, from the time that employees commence with the employer through to the end of the employment relationship.

In this chapter we will investigate:

- the implications of recruiting people from outside the European Union;
- the changes in the laws affecting how employers work with temporary agency staff;
- how to establish the employment contract;
- how to manage changing contracts and business transfers;
- the legislative foundation to managing employee rights;
- how to manage absence and health and safety;
- the process of managing redundancy.

Managing the start of the employment relationship

Recruitment and selection has become more complex with the freedom allowed to those in other member states to work in the UK and the complex immigration legislation developed by different governments. Employers' responsibilities have changed and it is important to understand these along with the process of recruiting from outside the European Union. We will start by reviewing anti-discrimination measure in recruitment and selection before exploring the legal recruitment of workers from overseas and the points-based system. Many employees start the relationship with an employer as a temporary team member, supplied by a recruitment agency, and so we will go on to review the impact of the Agency Workers Regulations 2010 (SI 2010/93). Finally we will give preliminary advice on preparing employment contracts.

Preventing discrimination in recruitment

We as HR professionals need to make sure that the actions of those representing the employer are fair and are not discriminatory during the recruitment and selection process. This means that all aspects of the process, from the job description and person specification, the preparation of advertisements, the short-listing and finally the selection process should be prepared with thought to prevent both direct and indirect discrimination.

Two cases have been chosen to illustrate the need for care in the recruitment and selection process. The first, in *King v Great Britain China Centre* (1991) IRLR 51, the post required 'a first-hand knowledge of China and fluent Chinese'. The claimant was Chinese and the successful candidate an English graduate in Chinese. The respondent was unable to demonstrate that the claimant had not been treated unfavourably and this shows that we need to keep clear records of the reasons for decisions so that employers can defend themselves effectively against a claim of discriminative recruitment and selection processes. In the second, *Rainbow v Milton Keynes Council* ET Case No: 1200104/07 (unreported), the issue was the wording in an advertisement which sought a teacher 'in the first five years of their career', and the claimant who had 34 years' experience, was rejected. It was found that the claimant had been subject to indirect discrimination as those within her age group would be likely to have more than five years' experience.

Positive action

An employer is able to support people with a protected characteristic who may be particularly disadvantaged thus enabling them to overcome that disadvantage, Equality Act 2010, s.159. Positive action can only be used in recruitment if it is possible to prove that people with the particular protected characteristic are under-represented or disadvantaged. Provisions can include targeted advertising or using the protected characteristic as 'a tie-breaker' when two candidates have the same merits. For further advice, the Government has produced a guide (Government Equalities Office, 2011).

Occupational requirements

Schedule 9 of the Equality Act 2010 describes occupational requirements. In some situations it may be necessary to recruit a person with a particular characteristic. For example there may be situations where it is necessary to recruit someone of a particular religion or sex, but in practice it is rare that an Employment Tribunal will look at this favourably unless it is clearly demonstrated that it is a proportionate means of meeting a legitimate aim.

Figure 4.1 on the next page shows a checklist for recruitment and selection.

Immigration and employment

Since the Coalition Government came to power there has been a policy to reduce net immigration and in particular non-European Union immigration. Though business requires skilled people it takes a fine balance in the way this is achieved using the skills of both current citizens and new immigrants to 'strengthen the economy' (Gower and Hawkins, 2013). This issue can become relevant to HR professionals as they recruit new employees and it is important that processes keep within the law.

The immigration process for the recruitment of nationals outside of the UK, the European Economic Area and Switzerland is complex, based on the Nationality, Immigration and Asylum Act 2006 and subsequent alterations to the Act. The explanation given here is to be viewed as a working introduction to HR professionals seeking to understand the process.

FIGURE 4.1   Checklist: Recruitment and selection – preventing discrimination

	Yes	No
1. Does the person specification only refer to requirements of the role which are clearly justifiable when referring to the job description?		
2. Can you objectively justify the reason why certain requirements are essential in the person specification?		
3. In the advert do you make sure that the words that are used do not imply that certain groups of people with protected characteristics are excluded or biased against?		
4. Can you explain how the choice of advertising media reaches a range of different people with different protected characteristics?		
5. Does your short-listing process use the job description and the person specification?		
6. If your application form asks candidates about any reasonable adjustments needed for the interview process, is this information removed before the short-listing process?		
7. Are all personal details that may provide information about the protected characteristics of a candidate removed prior to short-listing?		
8. Are all interviewers aware that they should not ask questions about a candidate's health or disability? (There are times when questions can be asked if the issues are fundamental to the role, but these are best completed by occupational health rather than an interviewer with no medical training.)		
9. Are all interviewers given specific diversity training?		
10. Are your selection methods justifiable? Do they test the requirements of the role?		

Responsibility for preventing illegal working

It is illegal to employ someone who is not allowed to work in the UK. As s.15 of the Nationality, Immigration and Asylum Act 2006 states:

'*It is contrary to this section to employ an adult subject to immigration control if —*

(a) *he has not been granted leave to enter or remain in the United Kingdom, or*

(b) *his leave to enter or remain in the United Kingdom is invalid, has ceased to have effect (whether by reason of curtailment, revocation, cancellation, passage of time or otherwise), or is subject to a condition preventing him from accepting the employment.*'

An employer can be fined up to £10,000 as a civil penalty under s.15, or for those employers who knowingly recruit illegal employees, the employer may spend up to two years in prison (s.21(2)(a)(i) of the Nationality, Immigration and Asylum Act 2006). There is no legal requirement to make initial and ongoing checks on the immigration status of employees, but the consequences of illegally employing staff provides an impetus for most HR professionals and employers.

As employers we should check and photocopy original documents prior to employment – this should be carried out by all employers regardless of size and for all applicants. Certain documents show that the applicant has an ongoing right to work in the UK, with no restriction. These are called 'List A' documents. Other documents show that there are restrictions on the ability of the applicant to work and these are called 'List B' documents (see Table 4.1).

Different combinations of documents are also acceptable and these can be found in *The full guide for employers on preventing illegal working in the UK*, which is published by the UK Border Agency (2012a). This also provides photographs of the different documentation and immigration and endorsement stamps so that we are not duped by a fraudulent application.

The points-based system

The points-based system covers migrant workers from outside the European Economic Area and Switzerland (UK Border Agency, 2012b). People wishing to work in the UK who currently live in the European Economic Area or Switzerland are able to do so under the Immigration (European Economic Area) Regulations 2006 (SI 2006/1003). The points-based system is underpinned by a five tier framework (see Table 4.2).

Tier 2 applications

As an HR professional we will find that the majority of immigration claims will relate to Tier 2 applications – known to most employers as the 'work permit'. In practice we will be involved in the transfer of employees from within the company (Tier 2 intra-company transfers) or general applications (Tier 2 general).

TABLE 4.1   Documents to show an employee's right to work (UK Border Agency, 2012b)

List A	List B
A passport showing that the holder is a British citizen or citizen of the UK and colonies	A passport or travel document endorsed to show that the holder is allowed to stay in the UK and is allowed to do the type of work in question
A passport or identity card that shows that the holder is a national of the European Economic Area or Switzerland	A biometric residence permit issued by the UK Border Agency to the holder that shows that the person named in it can stay in the UK and can do the type of work in question
A residence permit, registration certificate or document indicating permanent residence by the Home Office, the Border and Immigration Agency, or the UK Border Agency or an European Economic Area country or Switzerland	A residence card or document issued by the Home Office, the Borders and Immigration Agency or the UK Border Agency to a family member of a national of an European Economic Area country or Switzerland
A permanent residence card or document issued by the Home Office, the Border and Immigration Agency, or the UK Border Agency or an European Economic Area country or Switzerland	
A Biometric Residence Permit issued by the UK Border Agency to the holder that indicates the person named in it is allowed to stay indefinitely in the UK or has no time limit on their stay in the UK	
A passport or travel document that is endorsed to show that the holder is exempt from immigration control, is allowed to stay indefinitely, has no time limit to the their stay or has the right of abode in the UK	

TABLE 4.2   Points-based system tiers

Tier	
1	Highly skilled individuals and entrepreneurs
2	Skilled workers with a job offer
3	Low-skilled workers for temporary labour shortages (no implementation date set – tier suspended)
4	Students
5	Youth mobility and temporary workers: people allowed to work in the UK for a limited period of time, and are typically working to complete incidental work or work experience

For both Tier 2 (intra-company transfer) and Tier 2 (general) applications we must complete a certificate of sponsorship and have offered a job to the applicant. The certificate of sponsorship, which is a reference number rather than an actual document, provides the applicant with points and should be given to the applicant so that they can use it on their application for entry clearance. To complete the certificate of sponsorship an employer must be a registered sponsor.

For a Tier 2 (general) sponsorship the employer will have determined the reason for the sponsorship shown below (see Table 4.3).

TABLE 4.3   Certificates of sponsorship

Restricted Certificates of Sponsorship	Unrestricted Certificates of Sponsorship
They have completed a resident labour market test	The job will have an annual salary around £152,000
	The job is on the shortage occupation list

Restricted Certificates of Sponsorship are for jobs where it is impossible to recruit from the UK. These are restricted in number, and from April 2013 to April 2014 the number was set at 20,700. If a resident labour market test is required, then the employer will need to show that they have been unable to recruit within the UK, having advertised the job nationally for a minimum of 28 calendar days.

In the process of determining the reason for the sponsorship, unless the job is paid more than £152,000, the employer will have identified the standard occupational classification code and the minimum salary for that occupation. This is also required for the Certificate of Sponsorship.

Employing temporary staff – the Agency Workers Regulations 2010

Using temporary staff has become more complex for employers since the Temporary and Agency Workers Directive 2008/104/EC was implemented into domestic law as the Agency Workers Regulations 2010 (SI 2010/93). Prior to the change the main issue that occurred at an Employment Tribunal related to disputes concerning which party, the recruitment agency or the end-user employer was the actual employer. The regulations ensure a more equal approach to agency workers and the main points are as follows:

- After 12 weeks, agency workers should have equal basic working and employment conditions as permanent staff (s.5). This relates to pay and working hours and rest periods, but does not extend to other broader conditions such as sick pay.
- Agency workers have a right to the same basic hourly rate and bonuses for performance or work done (s.6)(3).

In practice this means we should enable agency workers to have access to facilities (and job vacancies) from the first day that they work with the employer and that employment agencies have up-to-date information on the terms and conditions for permanent staff, so that if the temporary worker reaches the 12-week period then they are eligible for equal pay.

Section 10 of the Regulations provides for situations where the agency worker is given a permanent contract of employment prior to taking up the first assignment. This contract will state that the agency worker has no rights under s.5 of the Act, insofar as those related to pay, and the worker will be paid a minimum amount between assignments – this is known as the

'Swedish Derogation'. The rate of pay between assignments must be at least 50 per cent of the assignment pay, above the minimum wage and calculated using a reference period which is usually the previous 12-week assignment pay (Department for Business, Innovation and Skills, 2011a).

The Swedish Derogation was tested in the case of *Bray and anors v Monarch Personnel Refuelling Ltd* (2013) (unreported). In this case, agency lorry drivers had been given permanent contracts by Monarch Personnel Refuelling Ltd, a recruitment agency. They were hired out to BP but these permanent contracts meant that they were paid 70p an hour less than permanent drivers employed by BP. The agency workers made claims against the employment agency relying on the Agency Workers Regulations 2010. The Employment Tribunal judged that Regulation 10 could apply to repeated assignments with the same employer and not be restricted to agency workers who moved between client employers.

Establishing contracts

There are two types of contract that an HR professional may encounter or be asked to prepare. The contract of service is the employment contract whilst the contract for services is that provided for freelance workers or subcontractors. In this section we are principally concentrating on the employment contract. The employment contract is binding as long as:

- an offer has been made (verbally or in writing);
- this offer has been accepted (verbally or in writing);
- there is consideration of payment for work;
- there is an intention to make legal relations.

In Chapter 2 we discussed the implied terms of a contract but in this section we will focus on express terms within the contract of service. The purpose of the employment contract is to explain the job offer, the terms and conditions of employment and relevant employer procedures.

Acas (2009b) provides details of what, at a minimum, an employment contract should include:

- name of employer and employee;
- date employment and continuous employment started;
- type of contract (permanent, fixed term);

- job location;
- pay and whether it is weekly or monthly pay and how it is to be paid;
- any benefits including pension;
- working hours;
- holiday entitlement;
- job description/job title;
- probationary period if applicable;
- details of any collective agreements that directly affect the employee's conditions of employment;
- notice period given at the termination of the contract.

The employment handbook will provide details of the employer's policies and procedures, but some parts of the handbook may have contractual status. The employment contract should refer to the fact that the employee has been given a copy of the handbook and specifically what parts of the handbook are to be viewed as express terms of the contract. This is particularly important if we wish to alter the non-contractual parts of the handbook. The employment contract should refer employees to the handbook for details of the sick leave process and pay, pensions, discipline and grievance procedures along with appeal processes.

In *Harlow v Artemis International Corporation* (2008) IRLR 629 the issue of inclusion of express terms in a staff handbook was paramount. In this case the claimant was made redundant but not paid an enhanced redundancy pay as was described in the Enhanced Redundancy Policy on the intranet site, which had replaced the staff handbook. The claimant's contract had the term 'all other terms and conditions are as detailed in the staff handbook as issued to you and subject to its most recent update'. Despite the respondent, Artemis International Corporation, disputing that the policy was included, the claim succeeded.

The contract provides opportunity for the HR professional to identify and formalize a range of issues and it is prudent to seek legal advice when first developing the terms of a contract. We may think it advisable to cover for example, restrictive covenants or bonus schemes, depending on our circumstances.

Managing change

Employers need flexibility to ensure competitiveness and there are two areas that we go on to review now. Firstly we analyse the impact in law on the ability of employers to change contracts to meet these demands and secondly we look at the complex area of business transfers and outsourcing.

Changing contracts

Employment contracts are agreements by two parties, and as such should be changed only if both parties are in agreement. It is clearly practical to consult with employees in any event, but the need is not just sensible – there is a legal requirement for changes to be made by mutual agreement. So to change a contract we, as representatives of the employer, will need to consult with the relevant employee to gain mutual consent.

It is worth firstly identifying whether the change that is to take place has a contractual basis. Management can make changes in work processes and methods that are not part of the contract without the need for consultation. Some of the staff handbook may be non-contractual, and so be easy to amend without consultation.

In most cases the need to vary a contract does not just involve one employee, but a number, and in this case a more formal consultation is required, with Trade Unions being consulted (and negotiated with) as required. As Acas (2010b) suggests, employees are more likely to accept change if they under-stand the reasons behind the changes and are involved and listened to, and consultation provides the opportunity for this to be carried out. This is all very well, but in reality agreements tend to be made in such as way that it may be difficult to determine what has been agreed, let alone evidence it. This is why it is important to put agreements in writing, and once the change has been agreed the employee should receive notification within one month.

This is the ideal option but there are times when the needs of the business require a change that some employees are unable to adapt to or there are contractual changes that can be made without agreement. For example, when the term 'as amended from time to time' was inserted into a contract in *Cadoux v Central Regional Council* [1986] IRLR 131, Ct Sess, it enabled the employer to withdraw a non-contributory life assurance scheme. The employer will also have a contractual right to vary the contract by, for example, the insertion of a mobility clause. However the employer must have express terms in the contract, the terms must be applicable to the proposed variation and worded so that the employer has as much flexibility as possible. As we write the contract it is the HR professional who inserts a mobility (flexibility) clause into a new contract, so that if circumstances change and the employee is needed at another site it is possible to make the change without varying the contract.

We have already said that the law is there to protect the weaker party, and this is applicable in the case of flexibility clauses. Sometimes employers insert a flexibility clause into a contract that enables the employer to make changes to the contract – in the case of *Cadoux v Central Regional Council* [1986] the term 'as amended from time to time' gives that flexibility. However employers cannot insert a term into the contract that enables them to unilaterally make fundamental and major changes to the contract, particularly changes that may disadvantage employees.

Unilateral changes

If as the employer, we impose changes without gaining consent, the contract will have been breached. The employee then has a choice on how to respond:

- continuing to work;
- resignation;
- refusal;
- 'stand and sue'.

By continuing to work the employee is viewed as having accepted the new terms imposed by the employer. This acceptance means that the employee cannot then take action for breach of contract.

The employee can resign, if they believe that the change in terms is fundamental and goes to the root of the contract, and they would claim unfair dismissal (constructive dismissal). Constructive dismissal is covered in more detail in *HR Fundamentals: Employee Relations* (Aylott, 2014).

If the employee refuses to work under the new terms then the employer is likely to take disciplinary action. If the employee is dismissed they could make a claim for unfair dismissal. The employer would need to show that the reason for dismissal was a fair one, in terms of s.98 of the Employment

Rights Act 1996. Employers tend to apply 'some other substantial reason' and argue that there is a business need for the change.

The employee may 'stand and sue' which means that the employee works under protest whilst making a civil claim of breach of contract to the High Court or county court (for reduction in wages the Employment Tribunal does have jurisdiction on unlawful deduction on wages, s.23, Employment Rights Act 1996). By choosing to 'stand and sue' employees are relinquishing the ability to claim constructive dismissal. But they can claim breach of contract. In *Rigby v Ferodo Ltd* [1988] ICR 29 the employer unilaterally cut wages. The House of Lords held that this was a fundamental breach of the contract and that Mr Rigby was entitled to damages – the loss of wages. Whilst the employment contract existed Ferodo Ltd was liable for the loss.

If we wish to unilaterally change the contract, it could be terminated. The employer might choose to provide employees with notice of redundancy and then offer new contracts as suitable alternative employment. In this case if the employee refuses the new contract then an Employment Tribunal will need to determine whether:

- the reason for dismissal was redundancy (there needs to be a true redundancy situation as described by s.139 Employment Rights Act 1996);
- it was reasonable for the employee to decline the offer of alternative employment.

One final but important point needs to be made if the employer's variation has been a reduction in wages. It is automatically unfair to dismiss an employee for asserting a statutory right s.104, Employment Rights Act 1996 and so an employee dismissed for alleging that they have suffered unlawful deduction from wages will be able to make a claim for unfair dismissal. This right does not rely on the two-year right to claim unfair dismissal, but as an automatic right can be claimed from the start of the employment relationship.

Business transfers and service provision changes – transfer of undertakings (TUPE)

When an employer transfers its business, or part of its business, to another owner then the terms and conditions of the employees being transferred are protected. The relevant legislation is the Transfer of Undertakings (Protection of Employment) Regulations 2006 (SI 2006/246) which implements the European Transfer of Undertaking (Protection of Employment) Directive 2001/23/EC. This also applies to the transfer of service provision from one contractor to another.

Acas (2012b) puts this more clearly, stating that a transfer has occurred (and is subject to the Transfer of Undertakings (Protection of Employment) Regulations 2006 when:

- *all or part of a sole trader's business or partnership is sold or otherwise transferred*
- *a company, or part of it, is bought or acquired by another (if the second company buys or acquires the assets and then runs the business rather than acquiring the shares only)*
- *two companies cease to exist and combine to form a third*
- *a contract to provide goods or services is transferred in circumstances which amount to the transfer of a business or undertaking to a new employer.*

For a service provision change to be covered under TUPE the change must affect an organized group of employees whose work continues fundamentally unchanged after the transfer to the new service provider.

The case of *Spijkers v Gebroeders Benedik Abattoir CV* (1986) ECR 1119 helped to define a transfer as needing to be a transfer of a 'going concern' or 'economic entity' that has retained its identity. Therefore the sale of assets or combination of companies includes everything that would make this entity a going concern, including employees. A further case, *Süzen v Zehnacker Gebäudereinigung* (1997) IRLR 255 provided for the transfer of an activity to be included under the Directive and therefore the Transfer of Undertakings (Protection of Employment) Regulations 2006. This enables business contracts for services, for example catering or cleaning contracts, to be included under the Regulations and so covers outsourcing and other service contract transfers.

The Regulations protect the employee from being dismissed by the transferring employer or the receiving employer for reason of the transfer, unless it is for an economic, technical or organizational reason (ETO) (r.7 (1)). It also protects the terms and conditions of employees that are being transferred: employees are protected by the Employment Rights Act 1996 (r.104(4)(e)) from dismissal for asserting TUPE rights (ie asserting that terms and conditions should not be changed when the employer plans to change them).

There is the possibility of terms and conditions being changed if the change is for an economic, technical or organizational reason or a reason unconnected with the transfer (r.5(5)) but in this case the reason for the change must include changes in the workforce – changes in job functions or the size of the workforce. Reasons that could be viewed under the ETO defence are, for example:

- an economic reason – changes to pay or hours due to the business having made losses and therefore having to cut costs;
- a technical reason – changing the way work is carried out by introducing new technology, and having to dismiss transferred employees who do not have the technical skills;
- an organizational reason – a restructuring of business in order to reduce a layer of management for efficiency reasons or a move of work location as the business moves its headquarters.

The legislation surrounding transfers of undertakings and service provision changes is complex and is part of the Coalition Government's drive to reduce bureaucracy. The Government is currently reviewing TUPE legislation and proposes changes to reduce its burden on employers. The response to consultation by the Government (Department for Business, Innovation and Skills, 2013c) has defined the changes that the Government wishes to make, and these include:

- more scope to change terms and conditions of employees after a transfer;
- changes to work location will fall within an ETO defence;
- service provision change rules remain the same. (This means that it remains easier for employers to determine whether TUPE will apply.)

This is yet to become law in January 2014, and changes may be made as the legislation progresses through Parliament.

Managing a TUPE situation

The management of a TUPE situation is a complex and demanding one, in which the HR professional may be dealing with either a transfer out or a transfer in of employees.

Transfer out

In this case, current employees will be leaving employment to join another employer. The responsibilities of the HR professional in this situation are as follows:

- To provide accurate information for the new employer about the terms and conditions of the employees: the new employer will also need to be informed of the policies and procedures of the past employer, any discipline and grievance within the last two years and any litigation. This will need to be detailed so that the new employer is able to meet obligations to maintain these terms and conditions and take on any liabilities held in relation to these employees. Rules 11 and 12 of the Transfer of Undertakings (Protection of Employment) Regulations 2006 refer to this, but may be subject to future legislative change as part of the Government consultation. The transfer of pensions is covered under the Pensions Act 2004.

- To inform employees of the transfer: these are covered in rr.13–16 of the Transfer of Undertakings (Protection of Employment) Regulations 2006. This includes the employees that will be transferred and those colleagues that are not being transferred but whose jobs will be affected by the transfer. Rule 13(2) of the Transfer of Undertakings (Protection of Employment) Regulations 2006 states that employers must consult with employees, informing them: that the transfer will take place, when and the reasons for it; of legal, economic and social implications of the transfer for any affected employees; of any measures that will take place in connection with the transfer such as a reorganization.

If employees are not represented by a Trade Union then the employer will need to inform and consult with the employees' representatives, and will need to arrange for the election of such representatives.

At the date of transfer, the HR professional will remove the transferring employees from the payroll and send the new employer their P45s. As the employees are leaving employment all usual processes should be carried out and if exit interviews are normal practice they need to be completed – however there is no need to complete a reference. There is no legal requirement to transfer personnel files but it is good practice to do so. However consider the requirements of the Data Protection Act 1998 when doing so.

Transfer in

In this case the employer will be gaining new employees and the HR professional will need to:

- Contact the 'transferring out' employer and seek detailed information about the employees – a sample letter is provided by Chartered Institute of Personnel and Development (2012a).

- Ensure that they are able to fully replicate the policies and procedures being taken on, and they may need to discuss this with the HR professional of the 'transferring out' employer. For example, the operation of bonus schemes or pay scales may need further details.

- Consult with union representatives or employee representatives, and those employees that will be affected by the transfer, for example those that new employees will be joining. Rule 13(2) of the Transfer of Undertakings (Protection of Employment) Regulations 2006 also applies to this new employer. The new employees will also need to meet the new employer, and this may be carried out as a group or in individual meetings.

- If there are to be some vacancies, often due to the loss of some employees who do not wish to transfer over, then recruitment for these posts will need to be undertaken.

As with the 'transferring out' employer, if employees are not represented by a Trade Union then the employer will need to inform and consult with employee representatives, and will need to arrange for the election of such representatives.

At the date of transfer, the new employees will need to receive a letter confirming that the 'transferring-in' employer is now their employer and, as with any start of employment, they will need an induction.

CASE STUDY   Tendering in the charitable sector

A charity working with disabled people tendered for and won the contract to provide support for disabled clients in their own homes in Hampshire. The previous organization had 30 employees requiring transfer to the charity. Once the tender was confirmed the HR Director and CEO of the charity arranged to talk with all 30 employees, and also spoke with the Trade Union representatives.

The HR Director made contact with the previous provider to gain information about the 30 employees and it was agreed that the two HR professionals would meet to discuss the pay structure, as this was quite different from the charity's, and though the transfer was not with the local authority, the pay system was based on the local authority pay structure. The charity was concerned about the transfer of pension rights and the HR Director sought legal advice; the transferring employees would be offered the stakeholder pension that the charity's other employees were offered, matching the contribution that the previous employer had made. The information from the previous employer was delayed (and the transfer date had to be put back) but once the HR Director had gained all the information on the terms and conditions from the previous employer, it was clear that actually the terms and conditions were fundamentally similar.

This was quite a small charity, and the tendered service added a substantial number of employees to the team. Though it was considered to be important to the HR Director that the charity met its legal requirements and was protected from risk, the HR Director was concerned about the impact that this service would have on the other services that the charity undertook. In fact the communication with the existing team and the new employees enabled the transfer to go reasonably smoothly. The HR Director spent time on the induction and worked hard to integrate the new employees, but the fact that the new employees provided services in clients' homes meant that it was harder to do, and the nature of the service was distinct from the charity's other work. When the charity lost the tender two years later, three employees had transferred to other posts within the charity, but the remaining employees transferred on to another organization.

Managing people

In this section we review three areas of HR responsibility. Firstly we look at the impact of discrimination legislation: we look at how to recruit and select employees and briefly consider how to manage employees fairly in employment. We then go on to look at managing absence (we will look in more detail at managing short- and long-term absence in the following chapter but here we discuss the practicalities of statutory sick pay and fit notes).

Finally we look at health and safety, which can often be part of the HR professional's remit.

Discrimination – Equality Act 2010

We have briefly mentioned the Equality Act 2010 in Chapter 2, but here while giving it a more practical evaluation can only provide a brief overview. Taking a practical approach we look at discrimination during employment, starting with a brief overview of the key aspects of the Act.

The Equality Act 2010 harmonized a number of different pieces of legislation to protect people with a range of different characteristics found in the Equality Act 2010, s.4 and s.18:

- age;
- disability;
- gender reassignment;
- marriage and civil partnership;
- race;
- religion and belief;
- sex;
- sexual orientation;
- pregnancy and maternity.

There are two main types of discrimination which we will look at here – direct and indirect discrimination. There exist other types of prohibited conduct (such as associative discrimination, harassment and victimization, and discrimination by perception). Direct discrimination occurs when a person is treated less favourably because of a particular protected characteristic, Equality Act 2010, s.13 (1). An example of direct discrimination is when a woman is not selected for an engineering apprenticeship because women are not interested in engineering. Indirect discrimination is found in s.19 and occurs when:

- an employer applies a provision, criterion or practice;
- this puts (or would put) people with a particular protected characteristic at a disadvantage; and
- the employer cannot demonstrate that this is a proportionate means of achieving a legitimate aim.

An example of indirect discrimination is the requirement for all employees to work from 7pm to 10pm as this discriminates against women, who are more likely to have childcare responsibilities. We, as representatives of the employer, would need to demonstrate that this is a proportionate means of achieving a legitimate aim, that there is a clear business need which is appropriate and necessary, and that there was no alternative that would meet the business need.

Practical steps – preventing discrimination during employment

It must be ensured that the employer and those representing the employer do not discriminate against employees by given them disadvantaged terms of employment s.39(2)(a) or disadvantaging or restricting their access to promotion, transfer or training, s.39(2)(b). For example a younger worker in a similar role and with the same experience as an older worker cannot be given less pay, just because they are of a younger age (but length of service may be acceptable for employees who have been working with the employer for over five years and the employer believes there is a business need). Terms of employment will include:

- pay;
- hours of work;
- holiday pay;
- holiday entitlement.

Details of occupational pensions are not subject to the Equality Act 2010.

In the case of the *Ministry of Defence v Cartner* (2012) ICR D17, the employee was a female Chief Petty Officer serving in the Royal Navy, who sought promotion to the post of Warrant Officer. She failed and brought a case of direct and indirect sex discrimination. The Tribunal criticized the approach of the Navy, who did not interview for promotion but depended on the annual appraisal report. They also found that there was a provision that advantaged sea-going employees against those working predominately onshore which discriminated indirectly against women. Whilst this case has been returned to the Employment Tribunal for a re-hearing it remains pertinent to employers who may well use an appraisal prepared solely by a line manager as evidence for promotion. It also reminds us to ensure that criteria for promotion are not discriminatory.

In this section dress codes and appearance also have a bearing, and this can be illustrated in *Smith v Safeways* Plc (1994) UKEAT 185/93/0912 where Mr Smith was dismissed for having a ponytail when a female employee would not have lost her job. Whilst Safeways wished to promote a conventional image clearly one sex was treated unfavourably and was discriminated against. This continues to cause employers difficulty, particularly when dress codes impact on religious expression as in *Eweida v British Airways* (2010) IRLR 322 when the claimant wished to wear a cross or *Azmi v Kirklees Metropolitan Council* (2007) IRLR 211 where a teaching assistant wished to wear a veil.

Further information about discrimination is covered in Chapters 2, 5 and 7.

Absence management

Absence management aims to reduce absence levels by recording, measuring and controlling sickness absence. The role of the HR professional in absence management is:

- to attempt to reduce absence;
- to ensure that the employer's system of sick pay is not abused;
- to ensure that all those that are able contribute fully in the workplace;
- to provide support and flexibility to assist absent employees to return to work.

(Absence management is referred to in Chapters 4–7.)

The impact of sickness absence is costly on all involved. The average absence rate for employees is 6.8 days (Chartered Institute of Personnel and Development, 2012b) with the majority of sickness absence being of 7 days or under and the cost of absence is £600 per employee. However there is a discrepancy between private and public organizations (see Table 4.4).

The higher cost of absence in the public sector could be attributed to more generous sick pay policies and the fact that the public sector has higher long-term absence, which is more costly. The most common illnesses and injuries prompting absence are minor (colds, flu, headaches and stomach upsets), stress and mental ill-health, and musculoskeletal injuries and back pain. These conditions are common and we can influence the situation by early

TABLE 4.4   Measures of absence (CIPD, 2012b)

	Private	Public
Average number of days lost	6.6	9.0
% of absence of up to 7 days	72%	54%
% of absence of 8 days to 4 weeks	14%	20%
% of absence over 4 weeks	15%	26%
Mean cost of absence per employee	£513	£647

intervention and this can also have some influence on the employee's decision to return.

Causes of absence

Much sickness absence is genuine and at times employees may make a choice to attend work despite being ill. It is unclear whether this is always positive; attendance when sick can pass contagious illness around the department, thus producing a potential increase in sickness absence. However the choice to return to work while sick can be the first step in preventing a short-term illness becoming one with greater impact on employers, employees, their families and society.

Hansen and Andersen (2008) have a three-factor approach to the decisions that cause absence. This is similar to that given by Huczynski and Fitzpatrick (1989). These include:

- work-related factors (time pressure, relationship with colleagues, autonomy and control over work tasks);
- personal circumstances (financial situation, family life and psychological factors);
- attitudes (work ethic and commitment).

The factors influencing this decision are complex and inter-related but if we are to affect sickness absence we need to have an understanding of the factors influencing the decision to attend. Work-related factors can be influenced by the intervention of HR professionals and line managers, for example by dealing with harassment and bullying, or by improving job design.

Absence policy and procedures

According to Armstrong (2012) absence policies should cover:

- the method of measuring absence;
- the target for absence levels;
- the trigger for action on short-term absence;
- the circumstances that would prompt discipline action;
- the process of reporting absence to the employer;
- sick-pay arrangements;
- return-to-work interviews;
- other interventions to reduce absence such as flexible working.

In this section we will look at the process of reporting absence, sick-pay arrangements and a very brief review of interventions to reduce absence.

Reporting absence

The first seven days of sickness absence do not need to be medically reported, but employees will usually need to contact their employer. After this the employee must visit their GP who will complete what is known as MED3 form. This used to be known as a 'sick note'.

In April 2010 the use of medical certification moved towards a more positive use of the 'fit note' by means of the Social Security (Medical Evidence) and Statutory Sick Pay (Amendment) Regulations 2010 (SI 2010/137). Using the sick certificate a GP would confirm that the employee was not fit for work, with the reason and a date at which the employee should be fit to return or would need to apply for a new sick certificate. Using the statement of fitness for work or fit note the GP could state that the employee will be fit to work if the following advice is taken account of. They then would be able to select a range of four possible alterations to assist the return of the employee:

- a phased return to work;
- amended duties;

- altered hours;
- an adapted workplace.

Whilst employers do not have to accept the GP's advice, if they do not they are required to take the statement as if the GP had advised the employer that the employee was unfit to work. Advice for using the fit note is produced by the Department for Work and Pensions (DWP, 2013b).

We often record the reasons for sickness absence which are given on the fit note, so that we can identify trends and manage potential health problems. Some HR professionals code their absence on the HR information system to enable reports to be made. One such classification, SART, has been developed by the Health and Safety Executive (HSE) and the Institute of Occupational Medicine (IOM) and can be found on the IOM website.

Statutory sick pay

After a qualifying period of sickness absence of four days in a row, a minimum statutory sick pay is available for employees. Eligibility, exceptions and the SSP1 Form given to employees who are ineligible for statutory sick pay can be found on the Gov.UK website (Gov.UK, 2013f). After the qualifying four-day period an employer's legal requirements start, but most employers provide a company sick pay scheme that covers this period. Statutory sick pay is paid for a 28-week period after which the employee can claim Employment and Support Allowance or from October 2013 Universal Credit (rolled out from 2013 to 2017: Gov.UK, 2013e).

Occupational health and other services

Many employers have their own occupational health providers who will assess employees as and when the employer needs this carried out, and will give the employer (through the HR professional) advice on how to support the employee back to work. Some larger employers may have private healthcare provision or employee assistance programmes (EAPs) to provide early intervention to support employees.

A further development made as a result of the Black and Frost review (2011) is the Fit to Work Service pilot, based in 11 sites in the UK, which has tested a case-managed multidisciplinary support process for those employees in the early stages of sickness absence in an attempt to get them back to work quickly. The Government proposes to implement the Health at Work Assessment and Advisory Service in 2014, with GP referral after four weeks of sickness absence. This will be a state-funded service with access to occupation health assessment and case management. The effect this will have for occupational health services for individual employers is uncertain.

CASE STUDY   How employers can make a difference

As we have mentioned, the impact of sickness absence is higher for public sector organizations. We therefore give two examples of local authority initiatives that are making a difference to reduce absence. These were report by the Local Government Group (2010) and the Chartered Institute of Personnel and Development (2011).

Conwy County Borough Council

Conwy County Borough Council had noted that musculoskeletal injury and stress were the two main causes of sickness absence and they decided to take strategic action to communicate the value of employees and attempt to reduce sickness absence. To do this they promoted a range of initiatives including access to a back care advisor, rapid access to physiotherapy, discounted leisure centre membership and lunchtime physical activity sessions such as Nordic pole walking.

Funding for the scheme was difficult to gain, and it was necessary to argue the business case and to monitor and evaluate progress closely. The scheme is attributed with a reduction in sickness absence from 12.7 days in 2006/2007 to 10.68 days 2008/2009. Conwy County Borough Council has moved from being in the worst third of Welsh authorities to the best third (Local Government Group, 2010).

Kent County Council

Kent County Council has an absence level comparable to other authorities in the South East but has focused attention on both absence management and well-being initiatives. Its approach has been holistic in that it has attempted to provide programmes that cover physical, social, mental and economic well-being as well as health promotion and organizational well-being. Examples have included a team weight loss challenge, targeted support of people with diabetes or food allergies, a virtual gym and a well-being health check programme. To complete its strategic approach to absence Kent County Council has involved HR, line managers, health and safety, occupational health and learning and development professionals in these initiatives.

Whilst continuing their well-being initiatives as interventions to reduce absence they also made some progress on the reporting of absence, for example establishing email alerts for managers when an employee reached a trigger level for action on short-term absence, categorizing stress accurately and providing training to support line managers – not just on managing difficult conversations but courses to support managers to manage change in their teams and to develop their coaching skills.

It could be argued that this is a well-resourced set of initiatives and its impact has been very successful with a reduction of 41,000 days of sickness absence in a two-year period and a saving on absence of £2 million. It has also improved morale and commitment as shown through the satisfaction survey.

Health and safety

Though strictly not part of employment law, HR professionals can at times be viewed as having a responsibility for some health and safety issues. In smaller organizations the HR professional may be given the role of overseeing health and safety, often without a qualified health and safety officer on site. In larger organizations the role may be to represent the company at health and safety committees, to liaise between health and safety officers and occupational health, and to manage any liability or other people management issues that result from this. Finally some HR professionals have absolutely no involvement in health and safety, other than their responsibility as an employee.

The Health and Safety at Work etc. Act 1974 provides the foundation for health and safety in the UK. A brief summary of some key responsibilities of both employer and employee is given below, but this is not to be viewed as a complete summary of the Act:

- the need for a health and safety policy (s.2(3));
- the need for safe provision and maintenance of plant and systems of work (s.2(a));
- the need for arrangements for safe use, handling, storage and transport of articles and substances (s.2(b));
- the provision of information, instruction, training and supervision to ensure the health and safety at work of employees (s.2(c));

- the provision of a safe workplace and the provision and maintenance of a safe means of access to, and a way out from, the workplace (s.2(d));

- that employees have responsibility to take reasonable care for their own health and safety and that of others (s.7(a)).

This provides a basis for health and safety but in 1992 a range of legislation brought in widespread change. This was known as the 'Six Pack' and included six items of regulation:

- the Management of Health and Safety at Work Regulations 1992 (SI 1992/3004);

- the Manual Handling Operations Regulations 1992 (SI 1992/2793);

- the Display Screen Equipment (DSE) Regulations 1992 (SI 1992/2792);

- the Workplace (Health, Safety and Welfare) Regulations 1992 (SI 1992/3004);

- the Provision and Use of Work Equipment Regulations 1992 (SI 1992/2932);

- the Personal Protective Equipment (PPE) Regulations 1992 (SI 1992/2966).

The 'Six Pack' regulations with their amendments together made extensive changes to the workplace. The Manual Handling Operations Regulations provided for the need for reducing the risk to employees (r.4(b)(ii)) and therefore to provide manual handling training, and the Display Screen Equipment Regulations provided for risk assessments for workstations (r.2) (to some extent already covered by the Management of Health and Safety at Work Regulations) and for eyesight tests (r.5) and rest periods (r.4). The Workplace (Health, Safety and Welfare) Regulations reviewed basic issues such as ventilation (r.6), temperature (r.7), and lighting (r.8). When it comes to temperature, these Regulations state that temperature during working hours should be reasonable (r7.(1)) but it is the Approved Code of Practice (HSE, 1996) that clarifies this as at least 16 °C if the work is not strenuous and at least 13 °C if the work is strenuous. This is often an issue particularly within the manufacturing sector.

The Management of Health and Safety at Work Regulations 1992 (and amended version in 1999) were particularly influential as they introduced:

- a risk assessment to identify potential risks and to prepare by identifying both preventative and protective measures (the 1992 Regulations, r.3);

- particular measures for young workers (the 1999 Regulations, r.19) or pregnant workers (the 1999 Regulations, r.16).

In practice the Health and Safety Executive gives advice on how to get started with health and safety. If we work in a small organization we may be the person who needs to establish health and safety procedures, or we may be part of supporting what has been already established. If health and safety has not been covered in the organization then we will need to arrange for the following:

- to find a competent employee to train in health and safety;

- to write a health and safety policy (if you have more than five employees this is mandatory);

- to manage the risks in the business by carrying out risk assessments;

- to consult employees about health and safety at work, managing risks and any training they might need;

- to provide training, information and safe workplace facilities;

- to make sure there are first aid facilities and that accidents can be managed with the appropriate support;

- to display the health and safety poster where employees can see it – this is mandatory;

- to make sure the employer has adequate insurance.

(HSE, 2013d)

CASE STUDY   Birse Rail

Birse Rail provides specialist engineering services throughout the UK. In 2001 there were six reportable incidents and management decided to take a zero-tolerance approach to accidents, with the aim of reducing accident frequency to 0.2. This has been achieved by ensuring top management support, a training support for site managers, increases in staff to support health and safety issues and a commitment from employees.

The results of the initiative have been the reduction in incidents, a saving of management time investigating these incidents and increased client confidence. Birse Rail have been highly commended by the Royal Society for the Prevention of Accidents (RoSPA) Construction Sector Award. Despite annual costs of £135,000, Birse Rail believe that the reduction in claims and reduced time spent by managers investigating incidents and managing absence outweighs this cost.

(Health and Safety Executive, 2013a)

Managing terms and rights

In this section we will review the impact of law on equal pay and look at a range of rights including maternity, paternity, adoption, the right to request flexible working and emergency leave.

Equal pay

Despite the fact that men and women with the same skills and experience should be paid the same rate of pay there remains a gap between the equivalent pay of men and women. Across the EU-27 countries women's hourly pay was 16 per cent lower than that of men (European Commission, 2013) and in the UK the gender pay gap was 19.5 per cent (European Commission, 2013). Section 66 of the Equality Act 2010 deems each worker's contract to have an implied clause that ensures equality of terms. This means that equal pay claims can be made by either men or women, but it is generally taken up by female employees. We therefore have a responsibility to employers to protect them from these claims and ensure that there is equality of terms between men and women.

The Equality Act 2010 (and the Equal Pay Act 1970 that it replaced) provides three routes by means of which female employees can make an equal pay claim:

- like work;
- work rated as equivalent;
- work of equal value.

The Equality and Human Rights Commission has produced a Code of Practice which can also be referred to in equal pay claims (Equality and Human Rights Commission, 2011a).

Comparators

We need to understand the process of a claim so that we can protect the employer. For an Employment Tribunal claim to be successful a woman needs to compare her pay with that of a male employee to show that she is paid less. According to the Equality Act 2010, s.79, this male comparator needs to:

- be employed by her employer or an associated employer and be employed at the same establishment as her;
- be employed by her employer or an associated employer, be employed at different establishments but have common terms and conditions.

The Equality Act 2010, s.79 (9), describes an associated employer as a company which the former has control over or two companies over which a third company has control.

In *Pickstone v Freeman's Plc* [1988] IRLR 357 HL, a warehouse operative claimed equal pay for work of equal value with a male colleague who was a checker warehouse operative. However the employer argued that there were already male warehouse operatives and that the warehouse operatives should be her comparator. However the House of Lords held that Mrs Pickstone was allowed to choose her own male comparator. It is also acceptable for a claimant to choose her predecessor as a male comparator, *McCarthys Ltd v Smith* [1980] IRLR 210 ECJ. We therefore have to make sure that we have an objective reason, for example less experience, for a woman replacing a man in a role to be paid less than the man. If there is no objective reason then the woman should be paid the same as her male predecessor.

Pay

Equal pay does not refer solely to the salary that an employee is given but also includes the full extent of the remuneration package including holidays, company cars and overtime payments. Equal pay provisions relate to contractual benefits (benefits defined within the employment contract) rather than discretionary benefits (benefits which are not guaranteed) but covered by the Equality Act (2010).

In *Garland v British Rail Engineering Ltd* [1982] IRLR ECJ the claimant as an employee was entitled to concessionary travel rates during and after employment, but only men could retain their entitlement for their family. The European Court of Justice supported the claimant, and described pay as being consideration in the form of cash or in kind, given immediately or in the future. *Barber v Guardian Royal Exchange* (1990) IRLR 240 ECJ determined that redundancy payment and pension benefits under an occupational pension scheme were included as pay.

Like work

An employee's work is like that of her comparator if the work is '*the same or broadly similar and such differences as there are between their work are not of practical importance in relation to the terms of their work*', the Equality Act 2010, s.65 (2).

In *Capper Pass Ltd v Lawton* (1997) ICR 83 a female cook provided between 10 and 20 lunches for the directors. Her male comparators were assistant chefs who provided around 350 meals in the staff canteen. These were seen as broadly similar and so both female cook and male chefs were carrying out 'like work'.

In other situations proposed male comparators may have different duties, responsibilities or hours but it is whether these make the two roles materially different that will affect the decision of an Employment Tribunal. For example in *Morgan v Middlesbrough Borough Council* (2005) EWCA Civ 1432, a female primary school teacher failed in her attempt to claim like work with a male administrator.

The Employment Tribunal can order a contract to be changed to remove the inequity and order arrears to be paid covering a period of up to six years.

Work rated as equivalent

If an employer has carried out a job evaluation scheme (JES) and the role of the female employee and the male comparator have been rated as of equal value, then we need to ensure that both roles are paid the same. Job evaluation is '*a method of determining on a systematic basis the relative importance of a number of different jobs*' (Acas, 2010a: 7). *Bromley v H J Quick Ltd* (1988) IRLR 249 CA established the requirement for an analytical JES to be carried out, one which would assess the components of the two particular jobs in terms of effort, skill and decision-making.

In claims of 'work rated as equivalent' any claim can only be backdated to the date the JES was carried out.

Work of equal value

This third means of making a claim can be taken by a female employee who chooses a male comparator whose job is different to her own, but it is claimed by the woman that the roles require similar skills and ability. In *Enderby v Frenchay Health Authority and Sec. of State for Health* [1993] IRLR 591 ECJ speech therapists compared themselves with pharmacists working in the NHS. The European Court of Justice accepted that different collective bargaining agreements had led to a higher pay increase for pharmacists than for other professional groups. Whilst speech therapists and pharmacists undertake different roles it was accepted that they have similar skills and abilities.

Material factor defence

We can still have a defence for inequality if we can show that the difference in terms is due to a genuine difference rather than a difference of sex. It may be that the difference in pay might be due to better qualifications, higher output or being based at different sites. It is possible that market forces require that roles in one location are paid more than those in another, and this is the factor that has determined the difference in pay. Another material factor defence might be that the difference is due to higher payment for working unsocial hours.

Family friendly rights

The four main areas of family friendly rights are explored briefly below – those relating to a new child (maternity, paternity and adoption rights), parental leave, time off for dependants (emergency leave) and flexible working requests. (Changes to parental leave and flexible working provisions are also covered in the book's conclusion and family friendly rights in Chapters 5 and 6.)

Maternity, paternity and adoption rights

The main maternity, paternity and adoption rights are illustrated in Table 4.5.

If employees take ordinary maternity leave, paternity leave or ordinary adoption leave they have the right to return to their original job. They are also entitled to all the benefits of their terms and conditions except those

TABLE 4.5   The main maternity, paternity and adoption rights

	Maternity	Paternity	Adoption
Ordinary leave	Ordinary maternity leave of 26 weeks	1 or 2 weeks	Ordinary adoption leave of 26 weeks
Additional leave	Additional maternity leave of 26 weeks	Additional paternity leave cannot be taken before the baby is 20 weeks old. Between 2 and 26 weeks if the mother foregoes her leave	Additional adoption leave of 26 weeks
Pay	Statutory Maternity Pay of 39 weeks – the first 6 weeks at 90% of salary or SMP (whichever is lower). The remainder is then at the lower statutory rate	Statutory Paternity Pay of 39 weeks – the first 6 weeks at 90% of salary or SPP (whichever is lower). The remainder is then at the lower statutory rate	Statutory Adoption Pay of 39 weeks – at the lower statutory rate

relating to salary (they retain these rights in additional leave as well). If an employee takes additional leave then if it is not possible for the employee to return to their original job then they should be given a job which is suitable for them and appropriate for them to do under the circumstances, and on terms no less favourable as in the previous job. This is to account for the fact that the employer may need to recruit a replacement for an employee taking this extended leave.

Maternity rights

The Maternity and Parental Leave Regulations 1999 (SI 1999/3312) relate to the right to maternity leave. All mothers are entitled to both ordinary and additional maternity leave, but to access her rights to Statutory Maternity Pay a woman must:

- work for an employer who is liable to pay the employer's share of Class 1 National Insurance contributions;
- have an average weekly earnings above the lower earnings limit for the payment of National Insurance contributions;
- have 26 weeks' continuous service at the fifteenth week before the expected week of childbirth (EWC).

To be entitled to ordinary maternity leave the employee must inform the employer that she is pregnant and the date she expects to take leave (not earlier than the eleventh week before the EWC). This must be completed no later than the end of the fifteenth week before the EWC (r.4(1)(a)). She is also required to provide the employer with a MatB1 form from her GP or midwife (r.4(1)(b)). She can change her date in writing to the employer giving 28 days' notice.

There are other special rights that a mother has due to her pregnancy. She has the right to time off for ante-natal care (s.55(1), Employment Rights Act 1996). The employer also has a duty to carry out a risk assessment for new and expectant mothers (r.16 of the Management of Health and Safety at Work Act 1999).

Once notified, the employer will write to the employee stating her return date, assuming that she will take the full 52 weeks' leave. If she wishes to return earlier she must inform the employer at least eight weeks prior to the date she wishes to return. There is the ability for women on maternity leave to work for up to 10 'keeping-in-touch days'.

Paternity rights

To access his rights, a father will need to have worked continuously for the employer for 26 weeks at the fifteenth week before the EWC, and be the biological father or responsible for care. A father is entitled to take leave but is only eligible if he informs his employer of his intention to do so by the fifteenth week before the EWC. He should use the form SC3 available on the Gov.UK website (Gov.UK, 2013c). Paternity leave can start:

- at the actual date of birth;
- an agreed number of days after the birth;
- an agreed number of days after the expected week of childbirth.

It must finish within 56 days (eight weeks) of the birth.

If he wishes to take additional paternity leave then the employee will need to give his employer form SC7 and may also be asked for the child's birth certificate and details of the mother's employer. There is no obligation on the mother's employer to provide any details of when the mother returned to work, to verify the father's request for additional paternity leave. A father also has a right to 'keeping-in-touch days' and must give at least eight weeks' notice of the date he wishes to return.

Adoption rights

To access rights to adoption leave and pay the employee must have 26 weeks' continuous service at the fifteenth week before the week they are notified of matching. Adoption leave is available for individuals who adopt or couples, one of whom will be entitled to adoption leave and pay. Employees should inform their employer within seven days of being matched with a child and will need to provide the employer with the matching certificate. Adoption leave can start from the date the child lives with the adopter or up to 14 days before the child comes to live with the adopter. Again the adopter has the right to 'keeping-in-touch days' and must give the employer at least eight weeks' notice of the date the adopter wishes to return. It must also be noted that if a couple adopts a child, the adoptive father will also be eligible for paternity leave and pay.

Parental leave

Sections 76–80 of the Employment Rights Act 1996 implements the Parental Leave Directive (96/34/EC) and provides parents, with one year of continuous service, with the right to unpaid leave. They are entitled to 18 weeks' unpaid leave for each child born or adopted up until their fifth birthday (or eighteenth birthday for children with disabilities). The purpose of the leave is to provide care for the child and leave should be taken in whole weeks. Employees will need to give the employer 21 days' notice of the start date and this can only be postponed by the employer if they have a strong business case. Employees cannot take more than four weeks leave in a year.

Time off for dependants

The right to take emergency leave is stated in s.57A of the Employment Rights Act 1996. The provisions are for an employee to take reasonable time off (but this is not defined in the legislation):

- to provide assistance when a dependant falls ill, gives birth or is injured or assaulted;

- to make arrangements for the provision of care for a dependant who is ill or injured;
- because of the death of a dependant;
- because of the unexpected disruption or termination of arrangements for the care of a dependant; or
- to deal with an incident that involves a child of the employee and which occurs unexpectedly in a period during which an educational establishment, which the child attends, is responsible for the child.

A dependant is defined as a spouse, civil partner, child, parent or person living in the same household as the employee but not an employee, tenant, lodger or boarder, except for the first two categories when it also includes a person who reasonably relies on the employee. The employee should inform the employer of the need to take leave as soon as is possible.

In *Royal Bank of Scotland Plc v Harrison* (2009) IRLR 28 EAT the employee had two weeks' notice that her child minder could not cover a work day. She was unable to find cover, but was refused the day off as dependant's leave when she told her employer. She was disciplined when she took the day off. The EAT supported the claimant and held that the emergency does not have to be unexpected or sudden.

Further advice for the employer, particularly on what is 'reasonable time off', has been given in *Qua v John Ford Morrison Solicitors* (2003) ICR 482 EAT. In this case the employee had taken 17 days over a nine-month period to care for her son. In this case the EAT dismissed the argument to deal with each occasion separately but confirmed that the employer can take the number and length of previous occasions into account in determining what is reasonable and necessary. However the employer cannot take account of the need of the business. This should help us advise line managers as they manage these emergency leave situations.

Flexible working

Employees with children up to 17 years old (or 18 years old if disabled) and employees with caring responsibilities are eligible to make a request for flexible working and we need to ensure that we have policy and procedures in place to manage these. The Flexible Working (Eligibility, Complaints and Remedies) Amendment Regulations 2009 (SI 2009/595), states that flexible working requests can be made for parents of children up to the age of 17 (though other sources state up to 16 years of age). This right is available to all parents, whether they are biological parents or adoptive parents or carers of an elderly or disabled spouse, civil partner, relative or adult not a relative but living at the same address as the employee. The employee needs to have worked for their employer continuously for 26 weeks and not made a flexible working request in the last 12 months. Employee shareholders do not have the right to request flexible working but under the Parental Leave (EU Directive) Regulations 2013 (SI 2013/283), agency workers with service of one year returning from unpaid parental leave are able to request flexible working.

According to Acas (2011) the application must:

- be made in writing, stating that it is being made under the statutory right to apply for flexible working;
- confirm the employee's relationship to the child or adult;
- set out the employee's proposal and explain what effect the employee thinks this will have on the employer's business and how this may be dealt with;
- specify a start date for the proposed change giving the employer reasonable time to consider the proposal and implement it (this may take 12–14 weeks);
- state whether a previous application has been made and if so the date on which it was made; and
- be dated.

Though this means that we may reject applications that have not followed the procedure we may wish to take a less legalistic approach if we are to retain staff. An employee often makes requests when a situation has changed – when childcare arrangements have not been satisfactory or when they take on responsibilities for caring. These can be stressful times for employees and it may be that it is difficult to make other arrangements. In these situations we need to be understanding, whilst ensuring that we meet the demands of the business.

The right extends only to the request and employers may refuse the request on a number of grounds:

- the burden of costs;
- detrimental effect on the ability to meet customer demand;
- inability to reorganize work among existing staff;
- inability to recruit additional staff;

- detrimental impact on quality or performance;
- insufficiency of work during the periods the employee proposes to work;
- planned structural changes.

There is limited case law on the issue of flexible working. In *Commotion Ltd v Rutty* (2006) ICR 290 the EAT confirmed the right of an Employment Tribunal to look into the grounds that the employer asserts as the reason for refusing the request and to determine if the Tribunal believes these to be factually correct. This reinforces the need for any refusal to be objectively based.

Flexible working policy checklist

The checklist shown in Figure 4.2 gives the main points to cover in a flexible working policy. Not all of these checklist points are mandatory; some such as the right to be accompanied and the right to appeal are clearly part of statute whilst the use of a trial period is best practice and provides the employer and employee with a chance to try the proposed change out.

There are a few additional points to be made to add to the checklist. Whilst there is no statutory requirement to use a form to make a request, the use of a form makes the complexity of the information required more manageable. It may be wise to provide the manager who is carrying out the meeting with some guidance as to the different options available and to have had a discussion with them prior to the meeting. Though there is no statutory provision for the meeting to have more than one employer representative, you may wish to ensure formal meetings have HR representation. There may be particular types of flexible working that you wish to describe in the policy, such as career breaks, sabbaticals or study leave, and, especially if your policy is produced as part of an intranet or policy document for employees, you may need to mention other types of leave and direct employees to the relevant section, for example, maternity or paternity leave.

Other statutory rights

Working Time Regulations

The Working Time Regulations 1998 (SI 1998/1833) lay down minimum working hours, rest periods, annual leave and make special provisions for night workers including the requirement for health assessments (s.7). The

FIGURE 4.2   Checklist: Flexible working policy

	Yes	No
1. Does the policy provide for statutory requests only or does it go beyond statutory provision?	☐	☐
2. Do you clearly state who is eligible to make a request?	☐	☐
3. Do you state that employees can request to change hours, the times when they are required to work or location?	☐	☐
4. Does the policy give the frequency that requests can be made?	☐	☐
5. Do you give a form for employees to complete?	☐	☐
6. Do you explain that you will return the form if the request is not complete?	☐	☐
7. Do you acknowledge the request?	☐	☐
8. Do you invite your employee to a meeting to discuss the request?	☐	☐
9. Do you state that this meeting will be within 28 days of receiving the request?	☐	☐
10. Do you clearly state that they have the right to be accompanied at this meeting?	☐	☐
11. Do you pay both employee and companion for the meeting?	☐	☐
12. Do you notify your employee of the decision within 14 days?	☐	☐
13. Do you give your reasons for refusing a request?	☐	☐
14. Do you give a right to appeal?	☐	☐
15. Does your policy provide for the use of a trial period?	☐	☐

Regulations set minimum annual leave at 28 days (though this may include eight bank holidays) but it remains unclear how legislation deals with the carrying over of annual leave when sickness absence, maternity or parental leave is involved. The Government has yet to respond to the consultation on proposed changes. It also set working time at 48 hours in a week (measured over a 17-week period) unless employees have opted out. The Working Time Regulations 2002 (SI 2002/3128) make special arrangements for young workers who can only work eight hours a day (s.6(a)) and 40 hours a week (s.6(b)).

National minimum wage

The National Minimum Wage (Amendment) Regulations 2013 (SI 2013/1975) brought in the following minimum wages for the period 2013–14:

- The adult rate increases to £6.31 an hour.
- The rate for 18–20 year olds remains at £5.03 an hour.

- The rate for 16–17 year olds remains at £3.72 an hour.
- The rate for apprentices increases to £2.68 an hour.

These tend to be reviewed annually each October.

Right not to suffer a detriment

Sections 43M–47 of the Employment Rights Act 1996 provide for the right not to suffer a detriment, an act or failure to act which puts an employee at a disadvantage. These are wide ranging and include:

- when an employee has been summoned to attend jury service;
- when carrying out duties as a health and safety committee member or by bringing the employer's attention to a health and safety risk;
- refusing to work on Sundays for those employees who are protected shop and betting workers;
- refusing to comply with a requirement which would have contravened the Working Time Regulations 1998 or refusing to forego a right conferred by these regulations;
- performing a role as a trustee of an occupational pension scheme;
- performing a role as an employee representative;
- exercising the right to time off for study or training;
- making a protected disclosure under the Public Interest Disclosure Act 1998;
- requesting leave for family or domestic reasons;
- acting as a representative for an employee at a discipline or grievance meeting.

Managing the end of the employment relationship

This final section looks solely at redundancy. Dismissal and disciplinary and grievance procedures, which may also result in dismissal or resignation, are covered within *HR Fundamentals: Employee Relations* (Aylott, 2014).

Redundancy

Redundancy is a form of dismissal deemed as a fair reason in s.98, Employment Rights Act 1996. It is defined as having occurred (s.139):

if the dismissal is wholly or mainly attributable to –

(a)   the fact that his employer has ceased or intends to cease to carry on the business for the purposes of which the employee was employed by him, or to carry on that business in the place where the employee was so employed; or

(b)   the fact that the requirements of that business for employees to carry out work of a particular kind, or for employees to carry out work of a particular kind in the place where the employee was employed by the employer, have ceased or diminished or are expected to cease or diminish.

So redundancy occurs when the employer closes down, when the need for a particular job reduces or when the employer moves sites.

Process of redundancy

Most Employment Tribunal claims of unfair dismissal relate to the process carried out for redundancy, including collective and individual consultation, selection for redundancy, redundancy pay and suitable alternative employment. We will examine each of these in turn.

Collective consultation

Before any collective consultation, if the employer is making 20 or more employees redundant then the employer will need to notify the Insolvency Service Redundancy Payments Service using the HR1 form. Copies of this form can be found both on the Business Link and BIS websites. Employee representatives will also need to be given a copy of the HR1 form.

If there are a number of redundancies then the employer will need to consult with the Trade Union representatives. Section 188 of the Trade Union and Labour Relations (Consolidation) Act 1992 describes the minimum periods of consultation as being:

- When the employer plans to dismiss 100 or more employees they need to collectively consult for at least 45 days.

- When the employer plans to dismiss between 20 and 99 employees they need to collectively consult for at least 30 days.

The consultation is undertaken with the aim of reaching an agreement with the representatives and the employer should disclose in writing the following (s.188(4)):

- the reasons for the proposals;

- the numbers and descriptions of employees whom it is proposed to dismiss as redundant;

- the total number of employees of any such description employed by the employer at the establishment in question;

- the proposed method of selecting the employees who may be dismissed;

- the proposed method of carrying out the dismissals, with due regard to any agreed procedure, including the period over which the dismissals are to take effect;

- the proposed method of calculating the amount of any redundancy payments to be made to employees who may be dismissed.

If there is no recognized Trade Union, then employers will need to consult with elected employee representatives. This means that usually we will need to arrange for a fair election of representatives, determine the number of representatives and enable affected employees to vote in secret for who they wish to represent them.

Where there is no collective redundancy, there is no legislative duty to consult Trade Union representatives. However employers, usually the line manager as the employer's representative, must consult with individual employees and should be able to show that the employee has had an opportunity to discuss the reasons for the redundancy, the pool for selection, the criteria and any alternative employment.

Selection for redundancy

Employers are required to have consulted employees or their representatives about the selection criteria and selection pool. Identifying the selection pool is an important step as it includes (and excludes) individuals from the process. An employer will include all those employees carrying out the particular work that is being reduced in a particular department or location, and may also include subordinate roles if there is similarity.

Employers can choose to interview employees for the remaining jobs. Alternatively they can use selection criteria to select employees from the pool. The selection criteria are those factors which an employer will take into account to support them to make their decision on whom to select for redundancy. Each redundancy situation may be different, but it is important that the criteria is measurable and does not rely on subjective opinion. It is likely that the criteria will include:

- attendance records;
- disciplinary records;

- skills or experience;
- standard of work performance.

When preparing the selection criteria, it is important to ensure that no one group of employees will be disadvantaged. For example, using the 'last in first out' or 'LIFO' method may select younger employees and therefore put the employer at risk of an Employment Tribunal claim. It is important that absences that relate to disability or maternity leave are not included in the process of calculating individual scores as this would again be discriminatory (as was found for a woman whose maternity leave was included in *Eurocasters Ltd v Greene* EAT 475/88).

If there are any appeals regarding this process the employer does not need to show the accuracy of their scoring, but just that the selection criteria were fair and correctly applied to that individual. In *Boal and anor v Gullick Dobson* EAT/515/92 the Employment Tribunal found that it was not necessary for the employer to share the selection criteria scores with the employee.

Redundancy pay

Employees that have a minimum of two years' continuous service are eligible to get a redundancy payment. This is given as recognition of the stake an employee has in their job and the company, and this stake increases as employees have invested time into their job. Therefore these payments have both a length of service and age component and we need to calculate redundancy pay in light of these. We should provide employees with a statement of their redundancy pay showing how it has been calculated, and this may be incorporated into a letter which will also discuss the practicalities of the end of employment.

Suitable alternative employment

The issue of what is suitable alternative employment has caused employers some challenges. If an employee unreasonably refuses to take the alternative role, then they forfeit the right to a redundancy payment. Therefore the employer needs to determine if the alternative employment is really suitable and if the employee has been reasonable to reject it.

There may be issues with suitability if the alternative job is at a lower salary or has lower status, as when in *Taylor v Kent County Council* (1969) 2 QB 560 a headmaster was offered a position in a pool of mobile staff. There may also be issues if it conflicts with a preferred career pathway as in

Readman v Devon Primary Care Trust [2011] UKEAT 0116/11 where the claimant was offered a role as matron of a hospital when her career path and qualifications were in community nursing. The Employment Appeal Tribunal held that the desire not to hold a hospital role was sufficient to be a sound and justifiable reason not to take the role and the claim succeeded.

Conclusion

This chapter has the wide remit of putting employment law into practice in the workplace, from recruitment, through managing change, terms and conditions, people and the end of the employment relationship. It has attempted to cover the wide breadth that we as HR professionals have to manage, from recruiting temporary workers (and the impact of the Agency Workers Regulations 2010 (SI 2010/93)), to the redundancy process. It is a very practical chapter covering the complex areas such as when parts of businesses are bought or sold, or work tendered for is won or lost, which is covered by the Transfer of Undertakings (Protection of Employment) Regulations 2006 (SI 2006/246). It also looks at how to manage absence and health and safety responsibilities.

The next chapter continues this theme of law in practice to explore some of these issues further, with practical advice on communicating business transfers and arranging settlement agreements, looking at managing absence and health and safety in greater detail, and how to carry out job evaluation and support employees facing redundancy. However we finish by exploring redundancy in practice and flexible working policies.

CASE STUDY   Redundancies in a multinational corporation

A global distribution company had to restructure its business, requiring 80 employees in Germany and the UK to be made redundant – out of a total of 170 employees. HR had not been informed early enough and had been given just two months to complete the process.

Once HR were aware of the restructure they identified that 60 employees were based in the UK. This meant that they needed 45 days to consult with employee representatives. They identified that there were no employee representatives and arranged for an election. To encourage employees to put themselves forward as representatives, the company agreed to provide a one-day training course for elected representatives to be run by an outside consultant. This all took time and the process had already been running for two weeks.

The employer then started the consultation with the employee representatives who questioned the employee pool and the implications of German and UK law. HR had to explain that because they were unsure about the accuracy of certain records in the German office they had restricted the selection criteria to attendance, discipline, qualifications and experience. Though the UK HR team were responsible for the UK employees, as there was no HR presence in Germany, the company provided an HR professional with German law experience to help them with any aspects of the redundancy that would require application of German law.

HR had been preparing a spreadsheet to calculate payments based on age and length of service. At the same time the HR team prepared at risk letters to all 60 employees based in the UK. Once they had completed the consultation they prepared the line managers for the process of redundancy and their assessments.

HR arranged for the line managers to attend two meetings – one in London and one in Frankfurt – held by the same senior manager and HR director. At these meetings line managers were also given all the details that had been given to the employee representatives and they prepared to manage the response from employees at risk of redundancy. These meetings also helped train and standardize the line managers' assessment – they were given the selection criteria and each one was discussed. The grading levels for each one were identified and the line managers were given some possible cases to grade so that the HR director was convinced that the grading was consistent. Line managers themselves found the process difficult – not all supported the company in their decision and yet were having to carry out assessments on their own teams.

When they returned from the meetings the line managers (with HR support) met with the 60 employees that were at risk in the UK. Line managers from the UK and Germany then graded all 80 employees and then sent these grades back to the HR department, who could then identify the total employees to be made redundant. They liaised with the German HR professional, informing him of the scores of the employees and together they identified that there were 38 UK employees selected for redundancy. They prepared letters for those employees that had been selected for redundancy, with details of the redundancy pay, payment in lieu of notice and a small *ex gratia* payment. These letters were ready to be given to employees but it was now two months into the process.

With HR support the selected employees were told that they had been selected for redundancy, provided with the letters and given information about the company outplacement service. The process had taken more than two and a half months and in retrospect the HR team felt that they had been process driven. Whilst they felt that they had supported representatives and line managers, the HR team would have liked to have been able to give more time to supporting those being made redundant to manage the anger within the teams or support those remaining employees. It took some time to recover from the rushed redundancies and absence and retention rates remained higher for the next year than they had been the previous year. Whilst HR had protected the employer from unfair dismissal claims by carrying out a difficult redundancy programme there were many aspects they would have carried out differently.

How you do it

05

INTRODUCTION

As an HR professional you will be aware of the wide reach of employment law. Even before employment is offered potential employees have protection against discrimination and after employment has ended the impact of employment law extends to writing references. The relationship between the employer and employee is regulated by law, and therefore this chapter is very practical and wide ranging. In this chapter we will discuss and advise on how:

- to clarify the employment status of those that work for you;
- to gain consent to changes to employment contracts;
- to communicate business transfers to stakeholders;
- to arrange compromise or settlement agreements;
- to manage short-term and long-term absence;
- to challenge discrimination in the workplace;
- to begin managing health and safety;
- to manage maternity leave and pay;
- to carry out job evaluations;
- to manage misconduct disciplinary meetings;
- to support employees facing redundancy.

Managing the start of the employment relationship

Relationships within a business organization can be very varied. Some people will be recruited as employees, and will be given an employment contract. Others will become independent contractors, with a contract for services agreed. They may be agency workers, with the contract made between the recruitment agency and the business. To add to this complexity their contracts may offer them a range of flexible working, so they can be full-time or part-time workers, or work term-time only; they may share jobs with another worker; or their contract may offer them a total number of hours to work in a year, an annualized hours contract. When taking a legal standpoint the status of a worker is important – individuals with different types of employment status have different rights and the employer will have different responsibilities. Therefore the next section discusses the differences between an employee and an independent contractor.

Key issues – status

An employee is defined as '*an individual who has entered into or works under...*
a contract of employment, which means a contract of service or apprentice-
ship', Trade Union and Labour Relations (Consolidation) Act 1992, s.295(1) and Employment Rights Act 1996, s.230. However the definition for worker, which would include an independent contractor, is much broader. A worker is '*an individual who works under a contract of employment, or under any*
other contract whereby he undertakes to do or perform personally and work
or services for another party to the contract who is not a professional client
of his', Trade Union and Labour Relations (Consolidation) Act 1992, s.296(1) and Employment Relations Act 1999 s.13.

The rights of employees and independent contractors are different and broadly cover tax, vicarious liability, employment rights and an illegal contract. As HR professionals, we need to ensure that our responsibilities for employees and contractors are met and so it is important to determine the difference. Table 5.1 details this further.

As we can see there is a need to clearly define the status of workers and many HR professionals choose to use the Employment Status Indicator Tool (HMRC: n.d.). We now also have the status of employee shareholder where

TABLE 5.1   Rights of employees and independent contractors

	Employee	Independent contractor
Tax	Taxed as part of schedule E of the Pay-as-you-Earn (PAYE) scheme	Taxed as part of schedule D by annual self-assessment
Vicarious liability	Employers are responsible for the acts of employees carried out during the course of their employment	Employers have health and safety and certain common law liabilities but otherwise the contractor is responsible for their own actions
Employment rights	Employees are able to access employment protection rights (Employment Rights Act 1996) not all available to them on the first day of work. They are also protected against discrimination (Equality Act 2010)	Self-employed workers are protected against discrimination (Equality Act 2010)
Illegal contract	If the contract is illegal both parties' rights may be affected	If the contract is illegal both parties' rights may be affected

employers can offer their employees a minimum of £2,000 shares in their employer's business or that of a parent company, and in return employees waiver the right to claim unfair dismissal, some flexible working rights and a redundancy payment. This is a new status which has set criteria that must be met, with some tax implications: more details can be found on both the GOV.UK and HMRC websites.

Managing change

Change can be positive – a degree of pressure supports people to perform and some change makes jobs interesting. However the pace of change has increased and the changes to employment contracts and the impact that this has on employees may be particularly stressful. Employees can feel insecure and anxious and it is therefore important to manage this effectively. Communication is discussed in more detail in the companion book *HR Fundamentals: Employee Relations* (Aylott, 2014) but two specific situations will be covered here, changing contracts and communicating about business transfers. It is important that the employer is protected in both these situations, and therefore we also look at agreement compromise or settlement agreements.

Changing contracts – gaining consent

If we wish to change the contract of an employee we need to consult with the employee. We must inform the employee of the change that is proposed, the reason for those changes and listen to any alternative suggestions that they have. We will advise the line manager on whether it is best to have a team meeting to discuss the proposed change or to have a series of 1-2-1 meetings with individuals (see Table 5.2). It is possible that we would recommend a mixture of the two.

Communicating business transfers to stakeholders

Regulation 13 of the *Transfer of Undertakings (Protection of Employment) Regulations* (2006) puts an obligation on the employer (usually a Manager with our support), to consult with the representatives of employees, such as a recognized Trade Union. These employees will be those that are affected by the transfer-out. These representatives need to be told:

- that a transfer is being made;
- the reason for the transfer;
- the date of the transfer;
- the legal, social and economic impact of the transfer on the affected employee;
- any measures that the old or new employer will take as a result of the transfer.

The above details can be provided to employee representatives and if there are any measures to be taken the representatives need to be consulted. The new employer must also hold a meeting with the employee representatives, and often if there are particular measures that will be made by the new employer there may be more than one meeting – again this will be held by a Manager with our support.

TABLE 5.2   Comparing team meetings and 1-2-1 meetings when proposing changes

Advantages of team meeting	Disadvantages of team meeting
• Employees' questions are answered once rather at each 1-2-1 meeting • Questions can prompt other employees to ask questions • Gives the impression of the employer being open and honest • Employees may persuade each other that the impact on the team is minimal or to their advantage • Can be used to introduce the change before carrying out 1-2-1 meeting with individual • Efficient use of time	• Employees may form their view collectively rather than individually, possibly resulting in resistance from the team as a whole • Employees may not be comfortable asking questions in front of colleagues • Some employees may find the meeting distressing • Employees that are absent need to be contacted separately, and often hear second-hand from their colleagues

Advantages of 1-2-1 meeting	Disadvantages of 1-2-1 meeting
• An employee is able to ask questions in private • Employees' individual circumstances can be discussed • The employee without colleagues has less power to resist changes • The employer may choose to make different agreements with different employees • Helps individual employees to feel listened to • May reduce number of formal grievances received on this issue	• Time consuming • Have to repeat information at each meeting • If the 1-2-1s are used without a team meeting employees who have had the first meetings will talk to the others and this will generate gossip

There are no legal requirements to discuss the transfer with the employees themselves. However it is good practice to meet with the affected employees to present the transfer and to have ensured that a Union or Employee representative is present at this meeting. We must remember to ensure that those employees that are absent, whether on holiday, taking sick leave or maternity leave, are also informed of the transfer, and do not hear second-hand. Further 1-2-1 meetings with the Manager along with us as HR professional and the affected employee are also recommended. Unlike formal discipline and grievance hearings, when the employee has the right to be accompanied by a companion, there is no statutory right to be accompanied, but it is good practice that employees are offered the right, and often employees are accompanied by their Union or Employee representative.

Employees should be informed about the transfer as soon as reasonably possible. Any uncertainly and office gossip can have a detrimental effect on both morale and work performance. It also prevents employees attempting to get information from line managers, other employees or HR and shows that the company is in control of the situation. This is particularly important if a contract has been lost and employees could fear that further contracts could be vulnerable.

Settlement agreements

Compromise or Settlement Agreements are usually negotiated between the solicitor of the employee and the legal advisors of the organization in order to protect the employer from costly Employment Tribunal claims. The employee has to agree to a settlement agreement, which may by-pass other usual methods of managing performance or disciplining (and dismissing) an employee.

An employee will wish to –

- ensure that they have enough money to support themselves between jobs – six months' payment is often viewed as a good settlement (Landau, 2013);
- ensure a good reference in order to secure the new job;
- reduce the cost of any Employment Tribunal claim;
- reduce the risk of losing an Employment Tribunal – with no compensation paid;
- gain a reasonable settlement which is not so low as to encourage the employee to take the risk of an Employment Tribunal claim.

From our perspective it may be wise to offer a settlement agreement that is above the statutory minimum so that it encourages an aggrieved employee to settle rather than take an employer to Employment Tribunal. Taking the longer view this will save the employer money as they do not have to defend a court case, with the cost of legal advice and representation and the time of the HR professional accessing information to defend the case.

Managing people

Challenging discrimination

We, as an HR professional, might view our role as acting reactively to issues and problems. However there is more that we can do proactively to support the organization to challenge discrimination. We may monitor discrimination through analysing grievances, and we hope that there is no criminal act that needs reporting but the main way we can challenge discrimination is by our role in culture change.

Changing the culture

The culture of a business is a reflection of its values and practices. These values are based on unconscious assumptions, unspoken beliefs and perceptions which employees share about the way work is carried out. As employees join the organization they bring their own values which may or may not fit with those of the employer. If they are too incongruent they may not feel comfortable to remain in the business – an employee working for Greenpeace will have different values from those working for British Tobacco. An organizational culture at its best has the ability to include people but at its worst it builds cliques and *'constrains the entry and advancement of people who are different in appearance, attitude of behaviour from members of the dominant culture'* (Metz and Kulik, 2008).

According to Armstrong (2012: 125) values can be expressed in:

- care and consideration for people;
- competence;
- competitiveness;
- customer service;
- innovation;
- performance;
- quality;
- teamwork.

These values can change and this is where the HR professional is able to influence the culture to build one in which discrimination is unethical.

Often a culture change programme will change a range of expectations of which challenging diversity may be one part. It may be building a culture in which the organization will focus on the customer or building a reputation, adaptability or peak performance. These will filter down into the practices and activities. In particular the line manager is the representative of the employer, and employees will watch their behaviour to see what they pay attention to or agree is acceptable. New employees may be coached by the line manager and longer-serving employees may reflect the values of their manager. So the HR professional will need to build an influencing relationship with the line manager, so that where necessary they can support the line manager to change their values and behaviour to fit that of the organization. This may involve coaching and mentoring.

Along with all other employees, we can challenge discrimination when we experience it personally or see others experiencing it. However our position as a representative of the employer makes this a difficult position to be in and often it is better that others challenge discrimination. If HR professionals challenge discrimination it may be in situations where it is unnecessary to make too much of the issue but merely making the point is sufficient. For example, we can point out an inappropriate screen-saver which the next time they visit is no longer in use. Steps towards removing inappropriate 'artefacts' (the more tangible aspects of an organization that communicate the organizational culture) can effectively change the culture particularly reinforced gently by legal precedent.

It is important to note that changing the culture can be used as a defence to indicate that reasonable steps have been made to avoid vicarious liability for discrimination claims.

Grievance policies and procedures

Before discussion of grievance policies, it is important to see the formal grievance as the last resort in employee voice. Communication channels between line managers and employees need to be open, and employees able to discuss all issues informally with their line manager. It may be that discrimination can be identified in these discussions and with support by the HR professional the line manager can make sure that the team is aware of what the employer recognizes as acceptable behaviour. If communication with the line managers is not open, or has not been productive, the employee may choose to take a grievance to the HR professional. This is seen by employees as a difficult choice, as it may result in the employee being viewed as 'trouble-making' and many employees do not choose to take the issue further, so the employer cannot challenge discrimination as they are unaware of it.

HR grievance policies need to be transparent and trust needs to have been built with employees so that they are confident to voice problems. It takes some self-assurance to make a complaint, but if there are issues that need to be resolved formally this is the forum for this. To some extent this may be because the approach of HR professionals is to expect loyalty and dissent is seen as disloyalty. However we need to move towards an understanding that employees have different motivations, values and varied approaches to work and that the grievance procedure is there for employees to voice their opinions, which may be a challenge for us.

Employees must be encouraged to use both informal and formal methods to express complaints and grievances so that line managers and HR professionals are aware of discrimination issues. This encouragement can be made by building a transparent communication process where all information is easy to access, and the employer is viewed as open and transparent. Also employers need to promote a range of communication processes so that employees' voice can be heard. Finally the culture of the organization should be founded on respect for individuals.

CASE STUDY   Diversity in the Victoria Police Force

In many different countries including both Australia and the UK, changes in both demographics and attitudes towards diversity have shaken what were traditional public sector worlds. Metz and Kulik (2008) describe the problems facing the Victoria Police Force in challenging diversity in terms of gender.

Difficulty recruiting meant that the Police Force needed to attract women, yet their career pathway was different to that of men and their responsibilities limited. Community pressure in the 1980s and 1990s set about some small changes, but any further change was strongly resisted.

Personal injury claims

Injury at work can be costly to the employer, and we can often find ourselves, as HR professionals, seeking evidence from accident books and other sources to support our insurance company to defend any claims. An injury may be a:

- physical injury, such as a prolapsed disc causing back pain following lifting;
- physical disease or illness, such as asbestosis, caused by exposure to asbestos;
- psychological disease or illness such as depression due to stress at work.

For an employee to have a claim of negligence the employer must have had a duty of care, which has been breached and resulted in injury or loss. The employer's duty of care to an employee cannot be delegated to anyone else and is individual. Employers should take special precautions with those employees more susceptible to risk, for example if they have a previous back injury or mental health problem.

As HR professionals dealing with absence we may be involved in supporting an employee following a period of depression. We support line managers to implement the company's duty of care to support the employee without putting that employee under risk of further depression (regardless of whether their first bout of depression was caused by stress at work). This may mean support to return to work, but also the duty of care continues after return to work. The employee will be always at greater risk of depression and will not need to be subject to increased risk of this – the line manager should continue to be aware of this. When we have a disabled person, who has a condition that affects their day-to-day activities adversely and has had this for one year, or it is expected to continue for over one year, this risk is highlighted and it is easier for the line manager to remember not to put them in situations of greater risk. But with those who do not have a disability the line manager is likely to treat the employee as others, and to forget that they remain more susceptible.

An example of a breach of this duty of care was the case of *Walker v Northumberland County Council* (1995) ICR 702 (QB). In this case the claimant had worked for the defendant for 17 years. In 1986 he suffered a nervous breakdown due to stress caused from overwork. Several months later he returned to work and informed the employer that his workload would need to be reduced. The employer agreed to provide the extra assistance that the claimant sought and stated that this would be available as long as it was required by the claimant. But after only one month the assistance was withdrawn and by September 1987 the claimant suffered from a stress-related condition. Shortly after he suffered another nervous breakdown and was dismissed on the grounds of permanent ill-health. The High Court held that the defendant had breached its duty of care in relation to the second nervous breakdown. In withdrawing the extra assistance the employer had breached its duty of care owed to the claimant and was ordered to pay damages.

This case and others emphasize the risk of personal injury claims for mental health conditions and put an extra burden on us as HR professionals to protect employees from injury and employers from claims. The role of occupational health support can be particularly helpful, as we can gain advice and medical opinion which we then, as HR professionals, can give to support line managers.

We may find that we have an employee who has damaged their back lifting at work. After months we might get advice from occupational health and the GP that their condition is such that it is unlikely they can return to work in the foreseeable future, and we may dismiss the employee for being incapable of work. Despite following procedure we may find that we face an Employment Tribunal claim for unfair dismissal and a personal injury claim. Our role communicating with the employee prior to the dismissal may prevent these claims, but it is wise to be aware of the risks that the employer faces, regardless of following procedure. Neither of these claims may have foundation, but the employer will still spend valuable time dealing with them. However employers are protected against past personal injury claims as claims must be made within three years (Limitations Act 1980, s.11(4)).

Managing short-term absence

Short-term absence in particular is challenging. While there is a need to keep employees actively engaged in work there is also a need to ensure that employees are at home resting or gaining medical attention when necessary. Judgement is needed to determine the balance of employer and employee needs. If short-term absence becomes a more pressing issue then there is a further challenge. Any dismissal must clearly identify between issues of misconduct and incapability – do we believe that the absence is not due to illness (misconduct) or that the periods of absence cannot be sustained by the company (incapability to work)? It is important to ensure that

TABLE 5.3   Examples of Bradford Factor Scores

	Number of occasions (S)	Total number of days (D)	Bradford Factor Score	Traditional number of days
Employee A	5	10	250	10
Employee B	1	10	10	10
Employee C	5	5	125	5
Employee D	1	5	5	5

the employer will establish a level at which these absences will be investigated, for example at five days' absence in a three-month period. This is not a particularly effective approach as employees may see this as an entitlement, and may, in the above example, taken unnecessary self-certified absence of four days in each three-month period, totalling 16 days' sickness absence over the year without triggering any investigation. Alternatively the Bradford Factor Score could be used as a trigger with a level chosen at which investigation is started.

The Bradford Factor Index though a useful tool in the management of short-term absence is a recording and trigger mechanism only; it does not identify the reasons behind the absence. Employees with a chronic or serious illness or disability may take more occasions as sickness absence but these will be identified along with those employees who take unnecessary or non-genuine sick leave frequently. It also does not identify patterns of, for example, Monday and Friday sickness absence which should be dealt with long before the Bradford Factor trigger is reached. So it is clear that the Bradford Factor Index should be used as a tool, with thoughtful investigation once a trigger has been met and additional data analysis to determine patterns that fall outside of the trigger mechanism.

Dealing with short-term absence issues

The Government's state-funded health at work assessment and advisory service will commence in 2014, but as yet it is unclear as to how this will affect the role of the occupational health specialist and the relationship between the state-funded service and the need to investigate short-term absence. It is likely that this will continue as described below because the four-week prompt for the GP to refer to the service would not be met by a series of short-term absences.

Once an employee's absence has reached a trigger some investigation into the absence needs to be carried out and for many employers that may involve the occupational health specialist. There may also be circumstances when additional support or investigation is required, for example if an employee informs their line manager of a health issue which the line manager is unsure how to manage.

The employee will be given an appointment with the occupational health specialist who will discuss the reasons for the absences. They will then report to us on whether there is:

- any support necessary for the employee;
- a disability with reasonable adjustments to be made;
- any underlying illness or injury that needs a medical report from the GP;
- no reason why the absence level is so high.

If the occupational health specialist cannot identify any reason why the employee would need to take such extensive time on sickness leave then this may be an issue that needs to trigger the disciplinary procedure. Taking independent specialist advice the HR professional has been given no reason why the absence is so high and so an appropriate sanction could be given.

However independent specialist advice may:

- recommend reasonable adjustments for disability;
- provide practical support for line managers dealing with health issues they are unsure of;
- suggest the GP provide a report, identifying any support that is necessary and estimating the time necessary before the employee may return to work.

Smaller employers may not have the resources to employ or contract an occupational health specialist. They therefore depend on us to investigate thoroughly and sensitively, but the independence of the occupational health specialist is particularly important and something that cannot be replaced by the HR professional who is viewed by employees as representing the employer.

between two and six weeks. At this stage the occupational health specialist should ascertain the reasons for absence, any barriers for return to work, options for returning to work (including phased return to work) and determining whether a more detailed assessment is required. If there is no occupational health specialist this should be carried out by an impartial and trained person, such as an HR professional.

If a more detailed assessment is necessary this should be carried out by the occupational health specialist. Some employers provide benefits that enable employees to have rapid access to rehabilitation specialists, such as physiotherapists, and these are effective tools to reduce time away from work. Whilst NICE (2009) recommends a combined assessment with the employee, occupational health and the line manager, in practice this is rarely carried out and the assessment of employees is carried out with little line management intervention. This means that we are the facilitators in the work with the employee, and must maintain contact with the line manager, particularly if there are any supportive interventions that may promote early return. Of course we, along with the occupational health specialist, will ensure confidentiality and sensitivity.

It is important that a return-to-work plan is agreed between us as HR professionals, the occupational health specialist and the employee, but that the approach that is taken is supportive and positive. To set up this return-to-work plan, an assessment of the work environment needs to be carried out and this is where the HR professional can provide the occupational health specialist with relevant information about the tasks carried out using the job description and person specification – along with information from the employee and line manager. If necessary the occupational health specialist will carry out an assessment of the workplace, identifying any adjustments or modifications that will support return to work. The return-to-work plan should also include the level and frequency of interventions along with any psychological support required.

Those employees with a poor prognosis for return to work, such as those with recurring long-term sickness or previous, frequent, short-term absence, will need intensive intervention which may include:

- counselling to support return to work;
- referral to rehabilitation specialists;
- adaptations to work or phased return to work.

Those with a poor prognosis may also have particularly complex needs, with barriers to return to work, such as previous poor relationship with their line manager or performance issues, which may need discussion and resolution prior to return. Those with a better prognosis will of course need less intensive intervention to help them return to work.

Long-term perspective

As the absence continues the burden on the business to continue work without the employee becomes heavier, particularly if the sick employee is a key team member or the organization is small, and therefore the business is less able to sustain its support. From our perspective and that of the line manager there are some important and difficult issues that need to be thought about:

- What is the impact on the business of the absence?
- How long will the absence continue and for how long can the business sustain its support?
- Does the GP believe that full recovery is possible?
- What is the prognosis?
- Will the employee be able to return to the same job or should they be given alternative work?
- Is alternative work available and is re-training necessary or possible?

There are two important steps that need to be made during the management of employees on long-term sickness absence, and these are to request a GP medical report and to consult with the employee. This will enable the employer to take account of issues identified in *Lynock v Cereal Packaging Ltd* [1988] IRLR 511 (Personnel Today, 2007):

- the nature of the illness;
- the likelihood of it recurring or of some other illness arising;
- the length of the various absences and the periods between them;
- the need for the employer to have the work done;
- the impact of the absences on other employees;
- the importance of a personal assessment of the situation;
- the importance of consultation with the employee;
- the importance of appropriate warnings of dismissal if there is no noticeable improvement.

disability. An employee may claim that they have a disability and that reasonable adjustments could have been made to enable them to return to work. If the employer has not made reasonable adjustments the employee may claim both unfair dismissal and disability discrimination. Though *Tarbuck v Sainsbury's Supermarkets Ltd* [2006] IRLR 664 demonstrated that lack of consultation with an employee was not discriminative in itself, so long as necessary reasonable adjustments were made, it is common sense to consult with an employee in this situation.

Pay and benefit issues for long-term sickness

Many employers provide sickness absence payments above their statutory obligations. Once the statutory sick pay period is completed at 28 weeks the employee can claim Employment and Support Allowance, or introduced in October 2013 and only fully implemented in 2017, Universal Credit (Gov.UK, 2013e). Often once the contractual or statutory sick pay period is completed then employees may reasonably accept that their employment is less secure. However there is no specific link between sick pay and the dismissal of the employee and it depends on the specific situation of both the employer and employee. The prognosis of the employee's condition may be positive but the requirements of the employer may be so urgent as to need to replace this employee as soon as possible.

A further complication to the dismissal of an employee on the grounds of incapability is permanent health insurance. Permanent health insurance (PHI) provides a payment to the employee once the statutory sick pay (SSP) period has been completed and therefore employees are no longer eligible for SSP. However payment of PHI is a benefit of employment and if the employee is dismissed then the provision of the benefit ends. Therefore the dismissal of an employee with PHI can be viewed as unfair.

Absence is referred to in Chapters 4, 6 and 7.

CASE STUDY   Matty at Matinal

Matty had been working for Matinal Ltd as an administrator for four years when her marriage began to fall apart and her husband left her. She was a quiet private person, used to resolving her own problems but now she began to feel quite anxious. She was so worried about how she would manage to bring up her two children and hold down her responsible job that she felt physically sick most of the time. She was still managing to work full-time but she did not feel able to tell her colleagues or her line manager anything about her changed circumstances or how desperate she felt. Matty spoke to her GP who prescribed anti-depressant medication. For three months she managed to work with the support of her GP.

The company that Matty worked for was completely unaware of her troubles and her workload was increased. It was only when Matty took sick leave that the employer (the HR professional, the line manager or even her team) was aware of the problems that Matty was facing.

Her GP stated in the fit note that she would need three months off, and that it would be better if she had a phased return to work. Matty was encouraged to visit her team with her line manager (who had kept in touch with her) before she started work and when she did she began working 10am to 3pm for three days a week, and the HR professional advised the line manager that Matty should be given smaller, less complicated tasks. The line manager met with Matty on the first day to support her return to work, and they agreed together to take 10 minutes at lunchtime each Friday for Matty to talk to her. Matty felt very strange returning to work and she could not function like she used to, her concentration and patience were very limited and she tired very easily. But by mid-January Matty was able to adapt her work pattern to 10am to 3pm five day a week. She sought this pattern as a flexible working request which was positively received.

Managing terms and rights

Two practical issues are covered in this section – most of us will encounter maternity rights, as female employees become pregnant and take leave. It is important that we are aware of the process that needs to be taken to keep within the law and maintain links with the employee. Fewer of us, however, have experience of job evaluation schemes though they are common within the public sector and at least 20 per cent of UK establishments have at least one job evaluation scheme (Eurofound, 2009).

Family friendly rights – maternity

When it comes to managing family friendly rights such as maternity, paternity and adoption leave and pay, it is important to have a systematic approach to ensure that the responsibilities of both employer and employee are met. Family friendly rights are also referred to in Chapters 4 and 6. Figure 5.2 identifies the key points that both parties need to remember for maternity leave and pay.

Equal pay – job evaluation schemes

Job evaluation schemes are systematic methods of comparing the relative importance of different jobs so that it is possible to justify the pay given for a particular job. According to Acas (2010a), in order to make sure that job evaluation is seen to be fair it is recommended that:

- employee representatives and employees are communicated with;
- information is gathered thoroughly and systematically;
- employees have an understanding of the basis on which the jobs are being evaluated;
- evaluation is completed consistently.

An analytical job evaluation scheme is required for protection against equal pay claims. The job evaluation scheme will need to separately appraise the different characteristics required in a job – the skill, effort, responsibility and working conditions. Each characteristic will be broken down into key factors. For example, responsibility can be broken down into:

- the supervision of others;
- contact with others;
- maintaining the safety of others.

Each factor will be weighted according to the importance of this characteristic to the organization. For example, in a company that develops IT systems it may be that keeping in contact with key specialists is less important than the other two factors, whilst in an organization dealing with financial decisions supervision may be more important, and in engineering maintaining safety may be paramount.

Jobs are then analysed against this structure. In practice this usually involves a paper-based analysis of up-to-date job descriptions or interviews where necessary. This results in all jobs being given a particular number of points

FIGURE 5.2   Maternity leave

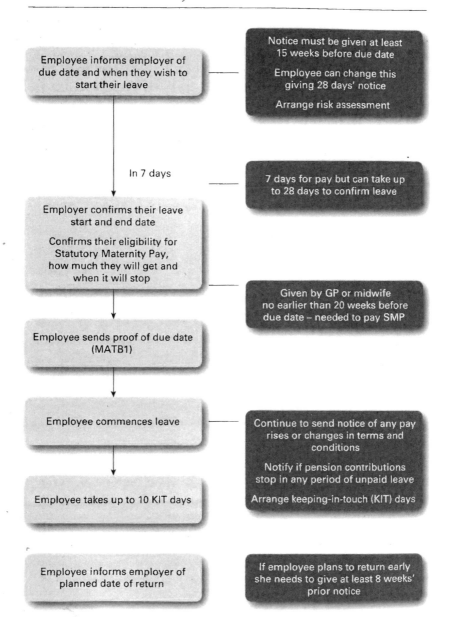

which then can be used to develop a grading structure. An important final stage is to carry out a gender impact assessment to determine whether the new grading system has an adverse effect on one gender and to decide how to remove this detriment if there is one.

CASE STUDY   Job evaluations

Two examples of standardized job evaluations are described here though there is no reason why a bespoke scheme should not be used by an employer. The first, the Greater London Provincial Council (GLPC), developed a pay spine in 2000 using a job evaluation scheme (London Councils, 2013). This has been used by a range of London councils and voluntary organizations (it is important to ensure that the scheme that an employer chooses is relevant to that particular employee). The GLPC broke down the factors required in a job to those shown in Table 5.4.

TABLE 5.4   GLPC factors

Supervision/ Management of People – 7 levels	Assesses the scope of managerial duties and the nature of the work which is supervised. Will account for flexible working patterns, deputizing, the number of staff supervised and their geographical dispersal.
Creativity and Innovation – 7 levels	Measures the extent to which the work requires innovative and imaginative responses to issues and in the resolution of problems, and the impact of guidelines.
Contacts and Relationships – 8 levels	Examines the content and environment of contacts required as part of the job. Measures the range and outcome of contacts.
Decisions	Operates as two sub-factors. **Discretion – 6 levels** – identifies freedom to act and the controls in place; **Consequences – 5 levels** – measures the outcome of decisions by effect, range and timescale.
Resources – 5 levels	Assesses the personal and identifiable responsibility for resources.

TABLE 5.4 *continued*

Work Environment Work Demands – 5 levels	Considers the relationship between work programmes, goals, deadlines and the subsequent management of priorities.
Physical Demands – 4 levels	Identifies a range of postures and demands of a physical nature.
Working Conditions – 4 levels	Examines the typical elements encountered with working inside and outside.
Work Context – 4 levels	Examines the potential health and safety risks to employees carrying out their duties.
Knowledge and Skill – 8 levels	Assesses the depth and breadth of knowledge and skills required.

Each factor has different levels and as the jobs are analysed the level of each factor will dictate the points given for that specific job. Once the job is analysed against the different factors each job will have been allocated points. These then show its relative value compared to the other jobs also analysed, and a pay scale or pay spine then can be developed.

The second well-used method is the Hay Group's Hay Guide Chart-Profile Job Evaluation Method (Hay Group, 2005). This method uses factors such as accountability, know-how and problem-solving (see Table 5.5).

Analysis against these criteria provides an assessment of job size and shape. Job size reflects the value of the job to the organization and is measured in the points gained from the factors. Job shape shows the proportion of the three dimensions, accountability, 'know-how' and problem-solving.

TABLE 5.5   Hays factors

Accountability	Every job exists to add organizational value by delivering some set of results (or outputs). Accountability measures the type and level of value a job can add. In this sense, it is the job's measured effect on an organization's value chain. It has three dimensions.

1 Freedom to act: The degree of empowerment to take action and the guidance provided to focus decision-making.

2 Scope: The business measure(s) the job is designed to positively impact.

3 Impact: The nature of the job's influence on business result.

Know-how	To achieve the accountabilities of a job requires 'know-how' (or inputs), which is the sum total of every capability or skill, however acquired, needed for fully competent job performance.

1 Technical/specialized skills: Depth and breadth of technical or specialized knowledge needed to achieve desired results.

2 Managerial skills: The requirement to undertake managerial functions, such as planning and organizing staff or directing and controlling resources, to achieve business results over time.

3 Human relations skills: The interpersonal skills required for successful interaction with individuals and groups, inside and outside the organization.

Problem-solving	The value of know-how is in its application to achieve results. 'Problem-solving' (or throughputs) refers to the use of know-how to identify, delineate, and resolve problems. We 'think with what we know', so problem-solving is viewed as utilization of know-how, and has two dimensions.

1 Thinking environment: The job's context and the degree to which problems and solutions are defined.

2 Thinking challenge: The nature of addressable problems and the difficulty in identifying solutions that add value.

Managing the end of the employment relationship

In practice, as expected, this can be a very difficult time, particularly if you know the employees going through a redundancy programme.

A brief review of misconduct dismissal

Whilst discipline and dismissal is covered more fully in *HR Fundamentals: Employee Relations* (Aylott, 2014), it is necessary to summarize this here.

Misconduct and gross misconduct

The Employment Rights Act 1996, s.98 enables an employer to dismiss on a range of grounds, including misconduct and incapability (this includes sickness, covered in absence and poor performance). Misconduct – illegal or improper conduct at work – is covered here and is a ground for disciplinary action. Examples of misconduct include unauthorized absence or lateness. More serious misconduct is known as gross misconduct, and these are issues of misconduct in which an employee may be summarily dismissed (dismissed legally without notice). Examples of gross misconduct include insubordination, fraud, being drunk or drug use at work. We as HR professionals will prepare a discipline procedure and this will list examples of gross misconduct (stating that these are not exclusive). While employees accused of incidents of gross misconduct may be dismissed summarily, they still need a fair process, with a genuine belief that they have carried out the act, on reasonable grounds based on thorough investigation. It may be necessary for the employer to suspend the employee on full payment whilst the investigation is carried out; this might be to protect the witnesses or to let tempers cool. Any suspension should be confirmed by us in writing and it must be stressed that it does not imply guilt.

Hearings

Initially, for less serious misconduct, the line manager will have an informal meeting. This is useful as it may uncover issues that can be resolved without resorting to the discipline process. For example, an employee persistently late for work may mention childcare problems, which with advice from the line manager, may result in a temporary change in working hours or a formal flexible working request. This example does not require the use of the discipline procedure.

If the informal meeting does not resolve issues then a formal hearing must be made. The employee will need to be invited by letter, and it is important that this letter:

- includes what is alleged;
- states the possible consequences of the action;
- gives enough information for the employee to prepare their case;
- gives information on the venue and time of the meeting;
- informs the employee of the right to be accompanied by a colleague or Trade Union representative.

At the hearing an appropriate manager and HR professional will attend, to investigate the issue. It may be that the hearing will reconvene later, or having heard the employee's case, a decision is made.

Warnings

It is preferable that the employee is informed about the result of a disciplinary hearing by letter. It may be that the issue is resolved by investigation and that there is no need for a warning to be given. However, dependent on the disciplinary procedure, there may be the option to give a formal warning, a first written warning, final written warning or dismissal. We need to send a letter informing the employee of the outcome, including the:

- sanction;
- change in behaviour required within a specified timescale;
- possible outcome if no change in behaviour is shown;
- right of appeal.

Cases of unfair dismissal

Employment Tribunal claims often refer to the case *of British Homes Stores v Burchell* (1980) ICR 303, EAT. This is important as it defines what an employer should do to dismiss fairly. An employer should have a genuine belief, based on reasonable grounds after reasonable investigation that the employee did carry out the alleged action.

Managing individual redundancy consultations

These are particularly difficult because as the employer you are both giving bad news to the employee with a possibly resultant strong emotional response.

Often line managers are concerned about carrying out these meetings because they have worked hard to develop a good working relationship with the team, which these interviews will alter, and they find giving potential bad news very difficult.

HR professionals need to support line managers by providing training and also ensuring that they sit in on any redundancy consultation. However much the HR professional wishes not to be involved this is when the employee needs the information that can be provided. Employees need clarity at this time so that they are able to make appropriate decisions and they are able to plan for the future. The HR professional can provide information about:

- the availability of voluntary redundancy;
- offers of early retirement;
- the process of redundancy including, if relevant, the way in which parties have been selected as 'at risk of redundancy';
- the options and process of applying for alternative work.

With a larger-scale redundancy programme the HR professional has a wider remit to provide support to improve job search, application and interview skills so that those employees that are being made redundant are able to find the appropriate job within the time frame that both the organization and the employee will require.

The role of the HR professional is to:

- support the line manager;
- provide addition information when required;
- ensure that employment law is adhered to and that employees are clear about the process.

In larger-scale redundancy programmes the HR professional will be able to support employees by providing job-search opportunities, development of links with recruitment agencies and re-training for interviews. It is usual that all discussions are followed up with adequate and clear written information concerning the process. By providing good-quality information to employees the HR professional is also managing their workload as it reduces the number of smaller issues that individual employees may ask the HR professional to explain.

Questions 1–3 relate to consultation and communication. For both employees selected for redundancy and those remaining after the redundancy programme, transparent processes and clear two-way communication is important.

Questions 4–9 are some of the methods that are available to employers to support employees selected for redundancy. Some might be emotional support, career advice or financial planning and it is recommended that this is carried out by an external and independent consultant. Other methods can be adapted for the different circumstances but show a commitment to those employees leaving and this is also communicated throughout the organization.

Questions 10–12 relate to line managers. When line managers get procedures wrong, and prevent an employee accessing something that the employer has offered, it can cause resentment and confusion. Reasonable time off for attending interviews is required by law under s.52, Employment Rights Act 1996. During this time employees may be attending interviews, and the sickness absence due to stress-related illness may also increase. Line managers need to allocate work fairly to reduce any anger and resentment that may be experienced by remaining employees.

Conclusion

The HR professional is responsible for ensuring that the employer acts within the law throughout the employee lifecycle, from recruitment and selection to dismissal and redundancy, or at the natural end of the employment. This section has attempted to touch upon a few of these areas to provide a foundation for the HR professional's practice.

CASE STUDY   Problems with Dave

There was a long stretch of walkway in the warehouse, and when no one more senior was around three of the younger workers would take chairs with casters on to race up and down the corridor. The new supervisor, Mr Jackson knew about it but thought it helped the team let off steam. He was called as first aider, when Dave's chair hit an obstacle, tipping him up so that his head hit the metal shelving. Dave cut his head and twisted his back, and after bandaging his head, Mr Jackson took him to Accident and Emergency. On his return, Mr Jackson completed an entry in the accident book.

Dave did not return to work the next day – his head was much better but he was finding it hard to move around because of his back pain. In the ensuing few weeks he had an x-ray and physiotherapy but his GP did not recommend that he return to work.

HR referred Dave to occupational health who assessed him and together they made a return-to-work plan, keeping in touch with him regularly. Though HR were aware that Dave was on sickness absence they were unaware that this was due to an accident at work until the health and safety officer emailed them (and this was confirmed by the occupational health report). HR followed this up with a discussion with the supervisor Mr Jackson and spoke to his line manager about whether disciplinary action was needed. HR also checked and placed a photocopy record of the relevant page of the accident book on Dave's personnel file.

Dave had been working at the company since leaving school two and a half years ago. The company had managed without him for a few months but it was beginning to get difficult and at four months' absence HR agreed to contact occupational health about the possibility of Dave returning to work in the foreseeable future. Then a personal accident claim against the company was received. This was sent onto the employer's insurance company and later the accident book record was also sent.

If the personal injury claim succeeded compensation for the loss of Dave's job would be included (this would be paid by the employer's insurance company). The fact that Dave contributed to his injury also added to the complexity of the case. The claim continued over many months and was not complete when occupational

Managing the start of the employment relationship

Short-listing

One of the areas that can be vulnerable in an employer's selection process is short-listing. Short-listing is the process of sifting through CVs and application forms to reduce the number of applications to select a smaller number to go through the interview process. At least two people should be involved in short-listing, usually us an HR professional and the recruiting manager, and they should:

- hold positions which are more senior than the one being recruited (ideally one should be a member of the team who is aware of team dynamics);

- be provided with the job description and person specification;

- have clear guidance on the criteria to use in rejecting or retaining applications;

- read the information in one sitting if possible;

- leave a written record of why each applicant was rejected or retained;

- have appropriate training.

A two-stage approach is useful in managing large numbers of applications, with initial screening against broad requirements. Then more detailed screening of a smaller number of applications can be made against more specific criteria. The use of a standard rating system can overcome subjective assessment of one application against another.

In *Tower Hamlets LBC v Quayyum* (1987) ICR 729 a Bengali social worker applied for a job as a team leader. The criterion for selection to interview was three years' experience, which the claimant lacked but the claimant argued Bengali applicants were less likely to achieve this. The claimant was not shortlisted for interview as they did not meet the selection criteria. This selection criterion was discriminatory and it is important when short-listing to make sure that we think through the implications of the decisions that we make.

Managing change

The management of change is a core aspect of our role as an HR professional. Change does not usually have distinct boundaries and clear definitions; it is often fluid and ill-defined.

As HR professionals we could take a planned approach to change, to look impartially at setting up new systems and processes or objectively at restructuring roles. We may be aware of the structured and logical theoretical models of change management and apply them to our work. Yet we know that in practice change that involves people will be complicated.

When we change contracts we can have a major impact on employees' lives and the outcome of the response of employees may depend on our prior relationship with them. We now look at how to make these changes go more smoothly by planning the communication.

Changing contracts – planning communication

In *HR Fundamentals: Employee Relations* (Aylott, 2014) we examine downward communication and here we look at this in a specific context – varying terms and conditions. The context for these changes are varied but managers are attempting to:

- bring to market new products and services;
- build products and services that stand out to their customers;
- reduce costs and streamline processes;
- restructure and integrate different businesses after acquisition or mergers.

The need to gain consent to a change in terms and conditions rarely occurs in isolation. It might be that a team will be required to change its method of working, changing shift patterns as a new product is manufactured or changing to service delivery after a new client contract is achieved. Or with a decline in business, the team needs to be streamlined and so members of the team might be required to take on a different shift pattern to manage a different workload with fewer employees. In larger organizations the change to terms and conditions may be part of a merger, which brings a torrent of changes itself including different management structures, different procedures, different products and services, different teams and locations. It is not possible to discuss the communication of large-scale, complex change but it is essential for us to recognize that the variation to the employees' contract is probably only one small but important change being experienced by the employee.

The aim of the communication is to gain consent to the change in terms and conditions with little 'collateral damage' ensuring that:

- the communication helps to improve the business performance;
- the talent is retained in the team to build the business;
- the communication maintains employee engagement and commitment to the employer and the team.

The main audience who will receive this communication is the team that will be affected by the change, the front-line employees and line managers. It is critical that we support those preparing to communicate the change to have some perception of the impact that change will have on employees – what their response might be. If we are to maintain the engagement of employees they will need more than an understanding of what is changing, but recognition that they deserve an explanation of the reasons behind it. They need to understand:

- the actual change itself;
- the business strategy and rationale;
- the impact on them as individuals and the team as a whole;
- the timescale.

Managing people

Enabling line managers to get the best out of their people requires that the employees are available for work and have the talent and skills that are needed. There is little law surrounding the acquisition of skills, other than ensuring that all, regardless of any protected characteristic, have equal access to training and development. We need to make sure that absence levels are improved, talented women return to work after maternity leave, that the best talent is available to our employer and that the environment keeps employees healthy, safe and able to work. Our role is to support and advise the line manager.

The practicalities of family friendly rights

We have already looked at some family friendly rights in Chapters 4 and 5 and in particular have discussed maternity, paternity, adoption leave and pay, and time off for dependants. We now look at the practical issues surrounding family friendly rights continuing the theme of maternity rights to review keeping-in-touch days.

'Keeping-in-touch' days

Maternity legislation has supported women to return to work, but despite this, some employers believe that ensuring that women return to the employer after the birth of their child, or stay any length of time in that role is problematic. However it has been shown that between 2002 and 2007 more women returned to their pre-birth employer, reducing the risk of employees having to take lower-paid or less-skilled jobs and retaining skill in the workplace for the employer (41 per cent of women had to change employer in 2002 and only 14 per cent changed employer in 2007) (BIS, 2010b). Keeping-in-touch (KIT) days, established in law by s.9 of the Maternity and Parental Leave etc. and the Paternity and Adoption Leave (Amendment) Regulations 2006 (SI 2006/ 2014) have helped to support this.

The birth of a child can be a world-changing event for a woman, particularly if it is their first child and issues surrounding the work–life balance can become a priority for those women managing a demanding job with a young baby. Yet women with demanding jobs are those with the talent that we particularly want to retain for the business. Business success depends on retention of skilled staff and keeping in touch helps to plan for employees' return to work more effectively.

An employee can work up to 10 KIT days for which she is paid her normal rate and which does not end her statutory maternity pay. Her maternity pay can be offset against her full pay or be additional to her full pay, but either way the employer will need to ensure that this is clear in the policy and clear to the employee taking the KIT days. If employees only receive the same payment as they would have if they remained at home on maternity leave it may not be enough to encourage women to use their KIT days and it may be wiser to pay any additional work on top of the Statutory Maternity Pay (SMP).

The employer (line manager) may find it difficult to bring an employee who has been on maternity leave, back in for an occasional day unless it is to carry out training. Someone else, a temporary employee, is carrying out her role whilst she is on leave, and though the line manager may have been in touch to some extent (as agreed with the employee) the employee may feel that she is not fully informed and therefore able to act as competently as before until she is up to speed. These KIT days are therefore essential in supporting her to return to work and we need to support the line manager to offer these KIT days.

It is important to note that a meeting of a few hours will constitute one KIT day, and the employee will be paid for the hours that they work. KIT days can be taken before and after the birth (though not in the first two weeks after the birth) and are not pro-rated for part-time employees.

The line manager and the employee will need to agree KIT days. The employer does not have to offer KIT days and the employee does not need to accept them. Though employees can work from home on projects for KIT days, and it may be useful for the line manager to bring employees back up to technical speed or to get a particular project completed, working from home does not help integrate employees into the company and their teams. The line manager may choose to invite the employee to join in training events, conferences or team meetings. As employees use their KIT days they can begin to experience what it may be like to return to work and it is more likely that discussions about flexible working happen earlier and more easily.

If we work in a larger organization, we may have procedures in place to record KIT days, but smaller employers may not. This could mean that errors are made with payment of KIT days, and it is advisable that the hours and days are properly recorded to ensure employees gain any additional payment. Employees should receive at least their statutory maternity pay and any additional pay if that has been agreed.

KIT days are a positive approach to integrating employees and attempting to retain their contribution. Time should also be taken to support women to return to work after the birth of their children.

Establishing a diverse workforce

In Chapter 4 we introduced the Equality Act 2010 and focused particularly on recruitment and selection and prevention of discrimination. In Chapter 5 we reviewed our role in challenging discrimination in the workplace. We now look at how we can establish a diverse workforce. We are not looking for a diverse workforce regardless of skill, but we want to ensure that the business has access to the full skills and talents in the market and that, once recruited, talent is used to its full potential.

Kandola and Fullerton (1998) describe a diverse organization using their MOSAIC model. This describes the diversity-orientated organization as having:

- **mission and values** – which are strong and positive and in which diversity will be a long-term goal;
- **objective and fair processes** – which are audited regularly so that no one group predominates;
- **skilled workforce: aware and fair** – with employees that understand how bias and prejudice works against the business and can prevent this happening and managers that concentrate on managing teams;
- **active flexibility** – flexibility in working patterns, policies and procedures to meet the diverse needs of its workforce;
- **individual focus** – an emphasis on individuals rather than segregating a group;
- **culture that empowers** – openness and trust with an absence of prejudice and discrimination.

The challenge for the HR professional is to translate this into the fabric of their own organization. The model that Kandola and Fullerton describe goes beyond compliance with statute and case law, and focuses on supporting organizational performance through the full use of human capital.

Diversity spans across the organization from the culture, mission and values of the organization, through policies and procedures that are objective and fair, improving managers' management skills so that they can manage different teams effectively and ensuring an understanding of law. We can tackle this by:

- working together in the team that have responsibility for policy development to ensure that these both meet legislative requirements and are objective and fair;

- ensuring policy and procedure on recruitment, selection, induction and appraisal fit the values of the organization, its focus on diversity and fairness;

- setting competencies or behavioural frameworks for employees that reflect the organization's value of diversity (along with the other values);

- training managers to manage in different circumstances and with different people: Thomas (1992) believed that managers did not have the managerial capability to manage diverse groups of people;

- monitoring and evaluating our activities to determine whether we have a diverse workforce: this will be covered in Chapter 7.

Planning to reduce absence

We have already looked at absence management processes (in Chapter 4) and then the specifics of managing short-term and long-term sickness absence (in Chapter 5). We now take a more proactive approach by looking at how HR professionals can reduce absence levels.

There are three different approaches that can be taken:

- the carrot (reward);
- the stick (punishment); or
- proactive intervention.

For example some industries have attendance bonuses that reward employees for attending work, or an end-of-year reward for not taking sick leave. These approaches now also have to take account of absence for maternity and disability reasons, which should not be included in any calculations of sick leave as that could result in a claim for discrimination. Other businesses do not pay sickness payment for the first four days of sickness – they are not required to pay Statutory Sick Pay (SSP) until the qualifying period has ended and can do this if it is an express term of the contract. They have strict and clear policies and will follow these to quickly dismiss employees for unacceptable absence levels. This approach can be effective for employers with tight staffing levels and low-skill jobs, which are willing to have a culture of compliance (eg Royal Mail Group), and we as HR professionals may make the choice to use this approach. These techniques can help to reduce absence but in this section we will concentrate on the proactive approach.

A strategic approach to reducing absence should be taken, with communication of the aims of the strategy. This is particularly important as employees will immediately feel that the employer is attempting to get employees to be at work when they are sick. It is more than controlling absence procedures tightly but will involve building a working environment in which employees enjoy participating and it encourages good attendance (Bolton and Hughes, 2001) and the approach taken will depend on the specifics of that particular industry and employer. The strategy should emphasize the role of line managers and the employee and their responsibility for their own health.

We have already identified three main aspects that influence absence – work-related factors, personal circumstances and attitudes. Work-related factors may include bullying and harassment, health and safety issues, excessive workload, mental health issues, and the lack of a career structure or poor relationships with managers. Here the employer can do a great deal to make the workplace somewhere an employee is happy to be. A large number of constructive dismissal cases involve periods of absence when employees remove themselves from, for example, sexual harassment. As the HR professional, we need to help the organization prevent this by ensuring:

- open communication;
- investigation and acting on grievances where relevant;
- training line managers;
- ensuring effective health and safety reporting;
- ensuring clear policies for bullying and harassment.

Personal circumstances include health issues, managing finances and family issues. Some employees will also have caring responsibilities. The tools that we may use to support employees to reduce absence may be any of the following:

- flexible working;
- counselling and employee assistance schemes;
- occupational health;
- well-being initiatives to cut smoking, promote exercise, eat healthily, manage stress;
- bereavement leave;
- health screening;

- subsidized gym membership;
- private medical insurance.

As we have mentioned, the approach needs to be targeted on specific areas of the business. A fast-moving and highly pressured environment will need the strategy to focus on improving psychological health; the NHS may prioritize psychological health but the physical nature of the work may also require a focus on health and safety reporting. The focus will depend on the business and the approach taken should identify the priority areas that will be tackled with the methods that will be used so that an integrated approach to health and well-being can be taken to reduce absence.

CASE STUDY   Positive examples

Well-being at Hillingdon Council

One of the key aspects for reducing absence is building a positive work environment with the HR professional taking a two-pronged approach – a strategic view on issues at work and enabling employees to take responsibility for their own health.

Hillingdon Council established a well-being campaign to reduce sickness absence and to ensure that employees were 'healthy, happy and here' (Pollitt, 2009). Integrating existing benefits they launched their strategy with an open day where employees could access support for finance, childcare and healthy living. Concurrently they improved their absence policy to make it more 'systematic and robust'. The number of days lost per employee per year has reduced from 15 to eight.

Yorkshire Ambulance Service strategy

A second example is that of the Yorkshire Ambulance Service NHS Trust which had a high absence level, the majority of which was musculoskeletal and stress-related. There were four strands to the strategy:

- your health – which included EAP and stress management;
- happy living – which included employee benefits and activities which would improve satisfaction, such as voluntary work;
- get active – which included physical and social activity;
- greener living – promoting carbon management.

This excellent programme reduced sickness absence by 33 per cent in the Emergency Operations Centre saving £500,000. Some of this paid for additional staff, thus improving the service so that the '*average 999 call answering times improving from 3 seconds to 1.5 seconds*' (NHS Employers, 2013).

Ensuring a healthy and safe workforce

In Chapter 4 we looked at how to get started with meeting the employer's health and safety obligations. In Chapter 5 we look at gaining advice and identifying risks. Now we review two practical areas that we and our HR team may be involved in – arranging training provision and reporting accidents and dangerous incidents.

Training provision

The Health and Safety at Work etc. Act 1974 and the Management of Health and Safety at Work Regulations 1999 refer to the provision of training and the employer's responsibility to ensure this is provided. We need to make sure that new starters have adequate training and that those who have been with the organization for a long time update their knowledge to keep their skills refreshed. If employees face new risks they may also need additional training. For example if staff are transferred from a manufacturing department to the warehouse, or from marketing to an on-the-road sales job, in both cases the risks will have changed and both new roles may involve greater lifting so manual handling training may be required. Specialist training may be required for:

- those starting a job – induction training to work safely in a new environment;
- those changing roles with a need for training for working with new risks associated with these roles;
- those taking particular health and safety responsibility within the company for training to carry out their role, eg completing risk assessments or fire marshal responsibilities;
- young employees whose experience of the workplace is limited.

Regardless of any special training for the company, all employers should evaluate what training is needed to support first aid provision. According to the Health and Safety Executive (2009) for those organizations which have low hazards (such as offices and shops) at a minimum an employer should have an appointed person responsible for first aid. This person will not have first aid training but will look after first aid materials and call the emergency services if required. With larger organizations or those with increased hazards it is recommended that a first aider is provided with first aid materials and a first aid room. This first aider will hold a First Aid at Work (FAW) or an Emergency First Aid at Work (EFAW) certificate and will need to undertake annual refresher training, as recommended by the Health and Safety Executive (2009). We will need to think through first aid provision to ensure that there are enough trained first aiders to cover holidays, absences and multi-site companies.

Reporting accidents and illnesses

Under the Reporting of Injuries, Diseases and Dangerous Occurrences Regulations (1995) (SI 1995/3163) (also known as RIDDOR), the employer should report for example certain accidents and occupational diseases to the Health and Safety Executive (HSE) and non-compliance is a criminal offence. This enables the HSE to monitor health and safety and to determine whether it is necessary to investigate further. Changes to RIDDOR (1995) made in October 2013 simplify the reporting of different injuries and occurrences. An employer must report:

- employee deaths or serious injuries;
- employee injuries that have resulted in absence from work for over seven days (not including the date of the incident);
- members of the public who have died or have been taken to hospital as a result of the accident.

(Employers must keep a record of those accidents in which employees are unable to attend work for three days, but do not have to report these.)

Certain occupational diseases must also be reported once an employer is in receipt of a diagnosis from the employee's GP. The conditions that are reportable are found in Schedule 3, Part 1 of RIDDOR (1995) and include occupational asthma resulting from exposure to specific pathogens, or occupational dermatitis. Most of these conditions are as a result of manual work, in the areas of construction, manufacturing or agriculture. Whilst every near miss does not need to be reported there are certain dangerous occurrences that must be reported, and these are found in Schedule 2 of RIDDOR (1995). These include dangerous occurrences such as those involving lifts, carriage of dangerous substances by road or collapse of scaffolding. If relevant the HR professional would be wise to check the specific occurrences on the HSE website or as part of RIDDOR legislation.

Whilst it can be seen that RIDDOR (1995) may predominate in workers in specific industries it is important for HR professionals to be aware of it. For example, if an employee twists an ankle in the car park or hurts their back when moving files in an office, then if they are unable to work for seven days or more these are reportable accidents. We can use the online facility to make a report.

All accidents at the workplace will be recorded in an accident book, but records of occupational diseases or dangerous occurrences may need to be made available to the HSE or local authority inspectors if they choose to investigate further.

Managing terms and rights

We need to protect the employer from equal pay claims and to ensure that we build a reputation that makes us one of the employers of choice for potential employees. A positive approach to diversity is part of this, but will involve some analysis of pay and benefits. In this section we look at the rights to equal pay and the responsibility of the employer to ensure that this is achieved.

Managing an equal pay audit

In Chapter 4 we looked at the Equality Act 2010 and described the three routes that an employee can use to make an equal pay claim. These were:

- like work;
- work rated as equivalent;
- equal value.

An equal pay audit or equal pay review is an investigation of the pay of men and women in the organization who are doing equal work. The causes of any inequality are also investigated and the gap closed in pay between men or women where there is no satisfactory explanation (Income Data Services, 2011: 395). The purpose of an equal pay audit is therefore to remove any inequalities of pay for men and women doing equal work and to protect the employer from claims, particularly those claims of 'like work'. (Those of 'work rated as equivalent' will have been identified as such through a job evaluation scheme and at that time the employer should have removed any inequality, but those of 'equal value' may be more difficult to determine.)

The Equality and Human Rights Commission in their Code of Practice and their online toolkit give a five-step approach to equal pay audits as follows (Equality and Human Rights Commission, 2009a):

- Decide on the scope of the review and identify data required.
- Determine where men and women are doing equal work.
- Collect pay data to identify equal pay gaps.
- Establish causes of any significant pay gaps and assess the reasons for these.
- Develop an equal pay action plan and/or review and monitor.

Scope of review

We have concentrated on equality issues between men and women but to fully protect the employer from claims of discrimination the organization should cover all protected groups. They should also cover all employees that are in the same employment or are paid from the same source. Section 79 of the Equality Act 2010 includes the same employer or an associated employer and at the same establishment or different establishments. As this equal pay audit is to be relied on to protect the company it is important that those who should be included are included, and for complex organizations it is necessary to get legal advice on this point prior to starting the review.

It may not be practical to carry out an audit on all employees and for all protected groups at one time and employers often make a decision to carry out the review in stages, undertaking a risk assessment to determine which areas should be reviewed first.

The review will need the support of top management. It may also be necessary to establish a project team with information on:

- pay and grading arrangement;
- any job evaluation schemes; and
- payroll and HR systems.

Data required

The Equality and Human Rights Commission has produced a comprehensive checklist of data (Equality and Human Rights Commission, 2009b) with explanations for the use of the different data gathered. The main details required are presented in Table 6.1.

TABLE 6.1   Data required for an equal pay audit

Pay	Personal characteristics
Base salary (FTE)	Employee number
Actual base salary	Job title and/or code
Bonus (annualized) and date paid	Job family
Other – eg pension, shift-pay, performance-related pay, all FTE	Band/grade/spinal point
Payments in kind – eg car	Directorate, dept., branch, etc.
Protected pay flag	Location
	Contract status
	Name
	Date of birth
	JE score
	Sex, ethnicity, disability indicator
	Date of birth
	Performance appraisal rating
	Date of joining organization
	Date into current job and/or Date into current grade

Collective agreements also need to be determined. We have already mentioned *Enderby v Frenchay Health Authority and Sec. of State for Health* [1993] IRLR 591 ECJ where different collective bargaining agreements had led to higher pay for the male-dominated pharmacists than for other female-dominated professional groups.

Protected groups and equal work

At this stage we will need to check whether men and women are doing like work, work rated as equivalent or work of equal value. When looking at men and women doing like work it is usual to look at job titles. These however can be misleading and it is important to compare what they actually do. Work rated as equivalent will have been rated under a job evaluation scheme and will need to be reviewed if the scores are the same or similar. Finally work of equal value will be measured by looking at effort, skill and decision-making. This is probably the most difficult area to rate and the Equality and Human Rights Commission recommend using an analytical job evaluation scheme which has been designed to assess equal value (Equality and Human Rights Commission, 2009c).

Collecting pay data

The data need to be checked for accuracy before those men and women doing equal work can be compared. Organizations often compare grades rather than individuals, if they are sure that their grades are free from bias.

We will then need to:

- calculate the average basic and total earnings for men and then for women;
- calculate the gap between average basic earnings between men and women;
- calculate the gap between total earnings between men and women;
- compare access to and amounts received of each element of the pay package.

We will need to record any significant differences (of 5 per cent or more) and any patterns of basic pay differences (of 3 per cent or more).

Areas of concern

It is important to be mindful of the fact that starting salaries may be different with men often appointed on a higher salary as they had a higher salary in a previous job rather than on entry qualifications and experience. Pay increases at promotion can also show bias. We might be concerned if we see that women have lower average earnings than men with the same job title or grade, or jobs in which women predominate are paid less than those in which men predominate. If this occurs we would wish to enquire further.

Causes of pay gaps

If there is a material reason for the difference in pay then there is no concern. We will need to check our pay policies to determine whether starting pay, pay progression, performance-related pay, bonus or shift-pay are designed or implemented in a way which would discriminate between men and women. After our analysis we may believe that there are factors within the policies that lead to sex-based pay, or our assessment may show that they are fit for purpose. Our analysis of the reason for the pay gaps may lead us to recommend a closing of these gaps.

Action plan

The final stage in the equal pay audit is to develop an action plan. If any pay gap cannot be satisfactorily explained then this will need to be closed, and equal pay provided as soon as possible. It may be that budgets need to be amended to enable those underpaid employees to gain equal pay, but the action plan should identify the timescale. The action plan should also identify the changes to pay policies that need to be made, and will ensure that the pay system is regularly monitored.

This systematic analysis seeks to determine whether there are any systemic biases or average discrepancies in pay between men and women and that the employer has improved protection having identified and resolved issues. The employer will still remain vulnerable to some individual equal pay claims that have not been identified.

Managing the end of the employment relationship

As HR professional, one of our responsibilities is to ensure that there are people with the skills needed when the company needs them. Yet salaries are one of the highest costs to the company and we may need to make redundancies if the needs of the business change. In this section we look at replacing staff that leave and planning large-scale redundancies.

Planning for replacement and retirement of staff

If HR professionals are to support organizational performance capability we need to have the resources to ensure that talented employees are available to meet demand. However with the removal of the default retirement age using the Employment Equality (Repeal of Retirement Age Provisions) Regulations 2011 (SI 2011/1069) this becomes more of a challenge. There were good reasons for the removal of the default retirement age including giving people the freedom to choose and removing age discrimination. However the knowledge that a talented member of the team was to leave at 65 years enabled businesses to plan for retirement and replacement. Whilst it is still possible to objectively justify a retirement age, in practice it is difficult to achieve and so in reality the certainty for employers has been removed.

Certainty when planning succession is always difficult – for people of any age might decide to move to a more challenging or higher-paid job, or when other circumstances mean that they need to leave our employment. Retirement is now just one of the many reasons that an employee may choose to leave.

Succession and talent planning

Succession planning is ensuring the availability of talented employees to meet the future needs of the organization. Employers may choose to select key senior roles and identify short-term and long-term successors for this role. Others may choose role pools, so that talented people can be developed to fill a number of roles. Talent planning is more general and is outside the scope of this book but here we look at succession planning and the link between senior roles and key employees.

We need to prepare for the future but 'one of the downsides of succession planning is the danger that a single leadership type will prevail. Studies have shown the unconscious instinct of us all to favour those who remind us of ourselves' (Kingsmill, 2010). This describes an inherent weakness in succession planning, where HR professionals need to ensure that the process is not discriminatory. In order to do this we can make sure that:

- the succession planning process is transparent;
- senior job roles are advertised so that all interested employees can apply;
- objective assessments of candidates are made;
- it is recognized that individuals plan their careers.

A transparent succession planning process communicates openly with those employees interested in progression – it ensures that they know how they are viewed, those roles they may be appropriate for and it actively encourages self-development (Chartered Institute of Personnel and Development, 2012g). All interested employees will be given opportunities to develop (regardless of protected characteristics) and should be supported. Succession planning can build expectations that the employer is unable to meet and so risks losing talented employees. However it also provides a career path that may retain able employees as they are developed.

CASE STUDY   Women in the boardroom

Diversity within the boardroom has been an enduring issue and has in the past concentrated on gender and equality. But, according to Deloitte Global Services (2011) the economic situation has moved from one of gender equality and the moral argument to one of productivity with evidence that a more balanced gender boardroom may improve productivity. Not only is increased boardroom diversity argued to improve productivity but research by Cohen and Huffman (2007) shows that when there are women in higher managerial positions the gender pay gap decreased in lower hierarchical positions, supporting improvements in equality throughout the organization.

In 2011 there was pressure on the European Union to set quotas on the number of women directors in the boardroom and Norway set quotas extending to 40 per cent female directors for boards of nine or more directors (Deloitte Global Services, 2011). Pressure for the European Union to set quotas has receded and European Union countries are focused on resolving the issue themselves – in advance of pressure again for quotas – as most countries prefer the soft-touch approach rather than quotas and sanctions for non-compliance.

In the UK, Lord Davies produced a Report in 2011 in which he criticized the poor level of gender equality in FTSE 100 companies, and a follow-up report was produced in 2013. It could be argued that major changes have been made in that *'the increase to date indicates that the rise in the number of female board members in just 18 months is equivalent to the increase in the whole of the last decade'* (Davies, 2013: 4) yet in the Spring of 2013 the number of female board members was only 17.3 per cent.

In November 2012 the European Union produced a draft directive which has been delayed whilst member states make other efforts. The directive aims for 40 per cent of women non-executive directors in listed companies by 2020. Lord Davies has sought support from FTSE 100 businesses to achieve 25 per cent by 2013.

Whilst we await the outcome, we as HR professionals, can support the initiative by reviewing the succession planning and talent pipeline for senior executives to ensure that diversity is encourage.

Planning a programme of redundancies

In Chapter 4 we reviewed the process of redundancy and in Chapter 5 we looked at individual and collective consultation. When we have a large number of employees being made redundant we may be able to call upon other support and in this section we examine the help that can be found.

The Rapid Response Service of JobCentre Plus can be very useful. It automatically contacts all employers who have used the Advanced Notification of Redundancies (HR1) to inform the Insolvency Service of 20 or more redundancies. The Government has a responsibility to ensure that people have skills to access jobs (Department for Business, Innovation and Skills, 2010a), and this assistance includes up-skilling or re-skilling people to improve their ability to take opportunities. The service can provide:

- careers advice;
- job-search and CV writing;
- benefit advice;
- identification of transferable skills and training needs;
- skill-based training and qualifications.

These can be provided onsite for large-scale redundancies, but the provision varies with the needs of the community, the employer and those being made redundant. Access to the provision depends on the effect that the redundancies will have on the local job market and the full service is only accessible once the employees are formally 'at risk' and will continue for individuals up to 13 weeks after they have lost their jobs.

Preparing for an Employment Tribunal

In Chapter 1, we looked at the Tribunal process including the hearing but here we look in detail at the preparation for a case. We may unfortunately find that we receive an ET3 and have to complete this within 28 days (the date it needs to be received by the Employment Tribunal is given on the letter from the Employment Tribunal). We may choose to respond online which means that the Employment Tribunal receives it immediately and there is no need to send a copy of our response form. If we do not return an ET3 the Employment Tribunal will review the ET1 and make a decision based on this alone. We need to provide sufficient detail but can only put into the ET3 what we can rely on as factual as this is the basis of our argument. It is important to remember that we may choose to accept liability.

The Employment Tribunal will have provided us with a case number which we will use on all correspondence with the Employment Tribunal and we will always copy the claimant into any correspondence. We will also make sure we have taken a copy of our ET3 before it is sent. If we have a legal representative they may choose to complete the ET3 – they will use legal language. However if we do not have legal representation our ET3 will have equal weight.

For further information please refer to the case study on developments in the Tribunal system in Chapter 7.

The preparation process

Our response form is sent to Acas who will contact us to determine whether they can help resolve the issues by means of conciliation. During that time we will gather all the relevant information, such as emails, letters or text messages from managers or other employees. There may be other relevant records that support the case which may need to be gathered, depending on the facts of the case. There may be documents that refer to employees not involved in the case, family members or children, and these may need to be made anonymous.

If there is a legal representative the case will be managed by them and they will contact us for the relevant information. If the employer chooses to represent themselves, then we will need to work with the employer (usually the company owner) to prepare the information. Along with gathering information we will gather witnesses, and at the same time we may find that current employees are called as witnesses for the claimant. This can be difficult and it is important that we support the process and ensure they are not put under any pressure. All witnesses (for either side) should be given time off to attend though it is not necessary to give them paid time from work, though it may be thoughtful to ensure witnesses for the employer are paid along with their expenses.

We may suggest that the employer and witnesses view an Employment Tribunal to look at the process and support them when they have to take the witness stand. Evidence from a witness who can be cross-examined holds more weight than that where the witness has been unable to attend. During the process the Employment Tribunal will also make orders, for example that witness statements are exchanged and the bundle agreed, and these will need to be complied with.

Bundle and witness statements

The information is gathered into a bundle, which should be indexed clearly so that the judge or panel can find the evidence easily. The bundle is often produced in a logical order, with the ET1 and ET2 followed by documents in date order. The witness statements may also refer to evidence in the bundle, with the reference page. This bundle should be agreed by the claimant and this is usually done by sending the index with details of the information and adding any document that the claimant wishes to be included. Correspondence to legal representative and 'without prejudice' letters (letters produced to try to settle the case) should not be included for the panel to read. Six copies of the bundle should be brought to the Tribunal so that there are copies for:

- the witness table;
- all three panel members;
- the claimant; and
- the respondent.

Witness statements should tell the story from the witness' point of view. Witnesses should be able to give evidence of your case and the relevant information involved, what they know rather than hearsay or conjecture. It is usual that witness statements are at least drafted by the witness themselves. Witness statements should start with the full name and address (business address) and should be signed and dated at the end of the statement. Each paragraph should be numbered so that it is easy for the witness or legal representative to refer to the appropriate paragraph. Witness statements are then exchanged so that the claimant is aware of the witnesses the employer will have and the case they will argue. This ensures that they are able to counter these arguments and that a fair hearing is carried out.

Schedule of loss

The bundle will include a schedule of loss prepared by the claimant. A full schedule of loss helps the employer if they are to make a settlement agreement. If we do lose a claim we will have the opportunity to provide evidence (this is known as a remedy hearing and is often heard after liability but may be heard along with this in the main hearing).

It is often wise to have prepared our response to the schedule of loss. For example if the claimant has not yet found another job, we may believe that the claimant has not done enough to mitigate their loss. We may provide a range of job advertisements that we believe the claimant could have applied for to argue that they should have been able to be employed at this stage.

Conclusion

This chapter has enabled us to look in greater detail at the practical aspects of the HR professional's role and to apply the law. Previous chapters have been able to provide legislation and case law for an HR professional to use to advise others. This chapter has related more to our own roles. We have reviewed aspects as diverse as short-listing, 'keeping-in-touch' days, strategic management of absence, equal pay audits and succession planning, providing discussion to support the HR professional in practice. In the next chapter we look at how we can measure some of the aspects that relate to employment law.

The case study below brings together change management and redundancy and examines how varying a contract is just one small part of change. A sales team is about to be restructured, with redundancies and changes to their work responsibilities. This involves a change in location but the contract does not give the employer the ability to change location without agreement.

CASE STUDY   Redundancies at Canton

Canton had manufactured contact lenses for sale to opticians throughout the UK for the last 10 years. It was viewed as reliable and had a reasonably steady customer base. It had recently acquired a small manufacturing company with experience in different contact lens technology, taking over its complimentary manufacturing lines and also developing another range of specialist contact lenses. Canton had the ability to expand but its sales and marketing team needed restructuring.

The current situation

The sales and marketing team in the UK were responsible for telephone contacts with opticians, attendance at conferences and regional marketing events with little or no individual contact with customers. The marketing team consisted of two employees and a small customer service team of five customer service representatives. There were five sales representatives who were based at three sites, London, Bristol and York, to be joined by a further six sales representatives from the new acquisition, based at the manufacturing site in Somerset. Canton had a good reputation which had been built up slowly so the lack of personal contact was manageable. A new approach was needed for the expansion and the sales support was inadequate. They also had too many sales representatives for the current sales model and these were based in the wrong locations. The existing structure is shown in Figure 6.1.

FIGURE 6.1   The existing structure

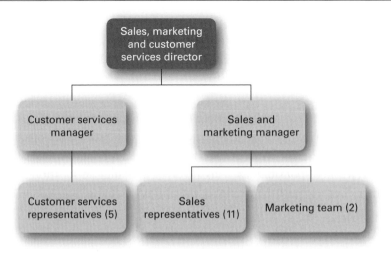

FIGURE 6.2 The new structure

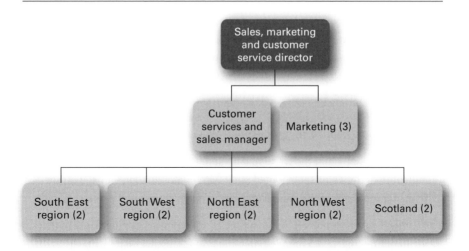

The project

It was suggest that sales would move alongside customer service, with one customer service representative supporting each regional sales representative. The team therefore consisting of five sales representatives and five customer service representatives. The marketing team would increase by one (see Figure 6.2).

This was a radical change for the team, both in terms of the reduction of the team from 21 employees to 15, and the change in the type of work. The sales representatives would need a good knowledge of both Canton's existing contact lenses but also those of the acquired company and the new specialist range that Canton was to launch. The location of the sales representatives was also problematic as the travel proposed with this new sales model would mean that three of the regions would be oversubscribed and two others, the North West and Scotland would mean that either two existing sales representatives would be required to relocate or that there would be need to recruit (and more redundancies would follow).

Implementation

This needed to be communicated to the team as soon as possible to prevent rumour as they were aware that many of the team did not have enough to do and that they were heavily weighted in the Southwest. As there would be about six redundancies there was no need for collective consultation, but it was thought wise to carry out a video-conference to communicate the proposed change to the team. The senior management team had identified the pool for redundancy as the sales and marketing team of 13, because at times all of these employees attended conferences and regional marketing events. Though only 11 sales representatives had talked with customers on the telephone recently, when the team was smaller there had been times when those in the marketing team had had to answer sales queries. Therefore it was thought wise to make a larger pool as they all had similar skills and experience.

Employees would need to know about the following:

- The project aim – that the UK would be segmented into large regions and members of the sales team would meet with customers individually rather than in large conference-based settings in major towns and cities.

- The business strategy – that these regions would provide customers with an identified business contact with whom relationships could be built.

- The rationale – that the business needed to reduce costs, to personalize business for customers and manage the expansion of a number of product lines.

- The impact – that both individuals and the team would be affected but that it would improve customer support and ultimately business performance. They would need information which would include a summary of the change in role, the new marketing role and the new structure of the team.

- The process – management would need to discuss the redundancy process, with identification of the pool at risk of redundancy and individual consultation meetings (further information on redundancy could be carried out later at the consultation meetings). They would also need to explain that all the sales representative roles would be internally advertised and those not selected for these roles would then face redundancy, unless they found alternative posts in the company. These new roles would have new terms and conditions as the previous roles were being made redundant.

- The timescale – management would need to discuss the degree of urgency of the project. The recruitment and selection process timescale would need to be clear (so employees knew the deadline for applications and possible interviews). They would also want to know the date that the redundancies would be made as this would provide information for them to plan their future.

This was communicated as a presentation by video-conference, with the opportunity for questions, and the marketing, sales and customer service director visited the sites in Bristol, London and York, with those employees based in Somerset coming up to Bristol for the day. With HR support the consultation meetings were carried out, but the director also made sure that employees were available to discuss the change informally and made sure that it was not only those at risk that were talked to – the customer services team also had questions and needed support. Over the three months of the process the director was visible with the team and made sure that employees were able to voice their questions and concerns.

The sales and marketing manager needed particular care. It was unlikely that Canton could keep the manager positive during the redundancy programme and after discussion with him it could be seen that his attitude was disruptive. The sales and marketing manager was placed on 'garden leave', as the terms and conditions of the contract allowed, prior to the redundancy. This removed the manager from the workplace enabling the director to support the team without the adverse comments of the manager.

This was a difficult change. In the end, seven sales representatives were made redundant along with the sales and marketing manager. One decided to take the new marketing role, and to develop a career in marketing. Those remaining were two Canton employees and one from the acquired manufacturer, retaining a mix of talent that supported the business.

Measurement

07

INTRODUCTION

The way in which employment law is applied within the organization can be measured by the number of Employment Tribunal claims that have been made against the company. Many of these claims ultimately fail and therefore there are problems using this as a measure. It would be preferable to deal with problems sooner rather than later, to avoid breaking the law. Measuring Employment Tribunal claims alone also assumes that when the law is broken employees will make an Employment Tribunal claim. This is not the case; some employees remain in employment and do not make a grievance or mention the issue whilst others leave. So we need other measures but most of the indicators that might highlight a problem are also influenced by other factors, hence we get an indistinct picture.

In this chapter we will examine:

- the role of the measurement of turnover;
- the way in which equal opportunities monitoring is carried out and can help reduce discrimination;
- the role of monitoring sickness absence in improving management and reducing claims;
- how the monitoring of accidents and incidents can be a preventative measure;
- how pay reviews are a final check in measuring equality;
- the way that HR professionals can carry out an audit.

The employment relationship

Measuring turnover and headcount

The measurement of the number of employees, both permanent and temporary staff, is known as 'headcount'. It is usually measured on a monthly basis and is used to show planned and unplanned changes in the number of employees in the department, site or organization. Drops in headcount that have not been planned show that employees are leaving of their own volition or as a result of disciplinary dismissals indicating problems of employee retention or poor discipline by managers. Planned headcount reduction through redundancy or through recruitment freezes (where employees are not replaced) are not measured as they are within the employer's control.

We should ensure that we keep a measurement of headcount, identifying significant reduction in headcount, particularly at department level. The reasons for leaving have been listed by Armstrong (2012) as:

- more pay;
- better prospects;
- more security;
- more opportunity to develop skills;
- better working conditions;
- poor relationships with manager or team leader;
- poor relationship with colleagues;
- bullying or harassment;
- personal – pregnancy, illness, moving away from the area etc.

Whilst some are 'pull' factors, attracting the employee away, others are 'push' factors. These are in the employer's control and could also indicate poor employment relations and possible risks of Employment Tribunal claims.

Turnover can be measured by using the crude turnover index:

$$\frac{\text{Total number of leavers over period}}{\text{Average total number employed over period}} \times 100$$

Another measure of turnover is the stability index, which focuses on those that remain and so looks at continuity of service. The stability index is as follows:

$$\frac{\text{Number of employees with n years' service at a given date}}{\text{Number employed n years ago}} \times 100$$

Grievance and discipline

It is worth monitoring both the number and issues involved in grievance and discipline. If employees are unsatisfied and believe that the law has been broken they may make a formal grievance. Monitoring these provides evidence of the employment relationship and possible compliance with the law. Employees that are subject to discipline should also be included – an increase in subordination or other misconduct, or unauthorized absence in a particular department, may suggest a problem needs to be resolved.

Managing people

It could be argued that managing people is the most significant when it comes to measuring law. The employer needs to makes sure that they operate within the law but also that employees believe that they are managed lawfully. For example, not all women who feel discriminated against during or after pregnancy will take their employer to an Employment Tribunal. However it is concerning that 31 per cent of the sample of 1,975 women questioned by legal firm Slater and Gordon felt that they had not been 'well treated' whilst on maternity leave, with 29 per cent believing they had missed out on promotion due to their pregnancy or the birth of their child (Sellgren, 2013). This increase in maternity-based discrimination is supported by other research and commentary, for example by Working Families (Working Families, 2013), though this may require more formal research.

We review four areas that can provide information for the employer to act upon and to be seen to act – equal opportunities monitoring, absence monitoring, the monitoring of accidents and incidents, and audits. What is important about these four areas is the fact that measurement is not sufficient and an employer needs to act on the information that the measurement provides.

Discrimination – equal opportunities monitoring

One of the more simple ways we can measure our organization's approach to discrimination and its effectiveness in reducing discrimination is by monitoring. Equal opportunities monitoring is the collection of information on the protected characteristics of employees or potential employees. It is particularly pertinent to the public sector but is good practice for all organizations, and in particular analysis and voluntary reporting of gender equality has been encouraged by the Government (Government Equalities Office, 2012).

Public sector organizations have particular responsibilities under the Equality Act 2010. The equality duty (s.149(1)) came into force in April 2011 and requires them to:

'a) *eliminate discrimination, harassment, victimization and any other conduct that is prohibited by or under this Act;*

b) *advance equality of opportunity between persons who share a relevant protected characteristic and persons who do not share it;*

c) *foster good relations between persons who share a relevant protected characteristic and persons who do not share it'.*

It covers age, disability, gender, gender reassignment, pregnancy and maternity, race, religion or belief and sexual orientation.

Public sector organizations must publish information to show how they are meeting the general equality duty and without adequate information they are unable to demonstrate this. Collecting information on equal opportunities will:

- help employers evaluate the impact of their policies and procedures;
- assess whether any of these are discriminating unlawfully;
- assist employers to make informed decisions about policies and procedures.

An employer will firstly wish to gain a profile of their workforce and may also wish to gather information that separates employees with different protected characteristics for the following areas (Equality and Human Rights Commission, 2011b: 5):

1 Recruitment and promotion

2 Numbers of part-time and full-time staff

3 Pay and remuneration

4 Training

5 Return to work of women on maternity leave

6 Return to work of disabled employees following sick leave relating to their disability

7 Appraisals

8 Grievances (including harassment)

9 Disciplinary action (including harassment)

10 Dismissals and other reasons for leaving.

This can be gathered by reviewing personnel records or by sending a questionnaire to employees or potential employees. These questionnaires should provide information to the recipient about how the information will be collected, used and stored and who will be able to access this information. (See Appendix A of the Equality and Human Rights Commission's publication for a copy of a sample questionnaire for general information and information covering promotion, part-time and full-time staff, and returning to work – this has been based on the census for 2011 so that generic answers can be compared with these national statistics.)

An example of a routine collection of information is that carried out by all job applicants who complete a brief equal opportunities questionnaire with their application. This can provide the employer with information about the number of people with a particular protected characteristic who apply for jobs and the proportion that are successful. It can give an indication of the effectiveness of, and any discrimination that may be occurring in, the recruitment and selection procedure.

The gathering of information about protected characteristics, particularly relating to sexual orientation, involves collecting sensitive data and so the Data Protection Act 1998 is also relevant. We might wish to think about the effect on the use of the information if data are inaccurate, as sometimes people are unwilling to release such sensitive data, and may answer falsely. The Equality and Human Rights Commission has provided a helpful guide, *Improving Sexual Orientation Monitoring* (Creegan, 2010) which can be found at: **http://www.equalityhumanrights.com/uploaded_files/research/ improving_sexual_orientation_monitoring_v6_22-12-10.pdf**

Data Protection Act 1998

It is necessary to give a brief summary of the obligations that the Data Protection Act 1998 places on employers as we are dealing with personal information. The Data Protection Act 1998 describes sensitive data as information that consists of the racial or ethnic background of an individual, political or religious beliefs, Trade Union membership, physical or mental health, sexual life or any offences that the person has committed. This therefore covers information gathered for equal opportunity monitoring, and the only two areas that could be viewed as non-sensitive are age and gender.

Schedule 3 of the Data Protection Act 1998 provides situations in which sensitive data can be processed. When dealing with sensitive data it is necessary that the person has given explicit consent (Schedule 3(1)) or at least one of the conditions of Schedule 3 are met. There is no legal requirement for sensitive data to be collected and so consent of the individual should be gained, particularly where the information given can be linked to that individual.

The Data Protection Act 1998 has eight principles to be found in Schedule 1 of the Act and these are:

1 Personal data shall be processed fairly and lawfully.

2 Personal data shall be obtained only for one or more specified and lawful purposes, and shall not be further processed in any manner incompatible with that purpose.

3 Personal data shall be adequate, relevant and not excessive.

4 Personal data shall be accurate and, where necessary, kept up to date.

5 Personal data shall not be kept for longer than is necessary.

6 Personal data shall be processed in accordance with the rights of data subjects.

7 Appropriate technical and organizational measures shall be taken against unauthorized or unlawful processing of personal data and against accidental loss or destruction of, or damage to, personal data.

8 Personal data shall not be transferred to a country or territory outside the European Economic Area unless that country or territory ensures an adequate level of protection for the rights and freedoms of data subjects in relation to the processing of personal data.

In summary this means that information gathered should be obtained, used for the purpose you have stated on the questionnaire and retained only for as long as is necessary. The employer should ensure that information is protected from unauthorized access or loss.

Using data

Once information has been gathered, it will be processed so that information is differentiated between the different protected characteristics. This can be compared to previous data, and variance between the previous data and the newly gathered data can be interpreted. If the information is available it can also be measured against published information from other similar employers, as other public sector organizations will also need to publish their information, either in their annual report or on their websites. This then can help us evaluate our policies and procedures to see whether they are discriminatory and assess how they can be improved so that the employer meets its obligations as defined in the Equality Act (2010) and is protected against Employment Tribunal claims.

Absence management – monitoring absence

We have already explained that employees take sickness absence for many reasons. Employees may decide not to come to work because, for example:

- they have a poor relationship with their manager;
- they have a pending disciplinary hearing; or
- they are experiencing sexual harassment by a team member.

Though we cannot identify individual issues from the measurement of absence, often claims of constructive dismissal are first identifiable as stress-related absence. Measurement of absence therefore gives an indication of the 'health' of the organization, and measurement of stress-related illnesses can also indicate problems.

Monitoring absence by department or organization can provide an imprecise indication of the state of the organization (as well as the health of the employees). A particularly high absence level in one department over a set period of time may have a number of different causes:

- a characteristic of the work is hazardous to health (employees may be short staffed and therefore work is particularly stressful);
- the manager does not have adequate training in managing absence;
- there are issues surrounding the management style of the manager.

Our role is firstly to provide absence information which can be compared at an organizational or departmental level. If we find a significant variance between our organizational absence level and that of the benchmark of other organizations in our sector then we may need to investigate further. If the level of absence between different departments varies significantly we will also be required to investigate the cause and put in measures to make improvements. Our investigation may lead us to improve absence by providing managers with training, for example in return-to-work interviews, but it may indicate a problem with a manager which may require a discussion with their more senior manager. Some action would need to be taken to support and train the manager and protect the employer from Employment Tribunal claims of constructive dismissal, discrimination, victimization and harassment.

There are some measures of absence that enables us to benchmark and evaluate absence within the organization. The Lost Time Index provides a measure of time lost by absence and can easily be transferred from a measure of time to an estimate of cost (though it does depend on the salary given to the absent employee and if at the time employees are highly paid the estimate will be less accurate). The measurement is as follows:

$$\text{Lost Time Index} = \frac{\text{Total absence (hours or days) in the period}}{\text{Possible total (hours or days) in the period}} \times 100$$

Health and safety – monitoring accidents and incidents

The monitoring of accidents and incidents, and the action taken as a result of these, can protect employers from insurance claims, and in some cases prosecution from the Health and Safety Executive.

Reactive monitoring is the monitoring of injuries, ill-health or incidents that could have caused injury or ill-heath, due to a failure in controlling risk. Commitment to and involvement in health and safety should see a reduction in accidents and incidents as risks are controlled. Reactive monitoring will involve:

- investigating accidents and incidents;
- the reasons for the accidents and incidents;
- failures in the health and safety management system;
- action to mitigate failures and prevent reoccurrence.

This is usually the responsibility of the health and safety officer, but in smaller organizations HR professionals will carry this out as part of their health and safety responsibility or we will have a role as part of the health and safety committee. In either case it is pertinent to recognize the responsibility employers have.

The case study below shows what could happen to businesses that ignore their health and safety responsibilities.

CASE STUDY   Cases of health and safety negligence

The three cases below indicate the cost of poor health and safety management, in terms of physical cost and harm to the employee and financial cost to the employer. Whilst the details of a case may have shown prior accidents or incidents, in general they show a range of failures, including lack of training, or the absence of risk assessment.

Fall from building site – Carillion and Febrey Ltd

Carillion was fined £130,000 and costs of £52,000 for breaches of the Health and Safety at Work etc. Act 1974, s.2(1) and s.3(1), after a scaffolder at a Swansea building site, in 2008, fell 19 metres, sustaining multiple injuries and resulting in his death two days later. Carillion was the main contractor, and had subcontracted some work to Febrey Ltd, who was responsible for this scaffolder. Carillion had identified failings in the health and safety management of Febrey Ltd but had been unsuccessful in gaining any improvement from Febrey Ltd.

The court found that Febrey Ltd had not trained its onsite management team and as a result the risk of at height working was not managed appropriately. It was also fined but had gone into liquidation. Its director pleaded guilty to a breach of s.37(1) of the Health and Safety at Work etc. Act 1974 and was fined £20,000 and ordered to pay £5,000 in costs (Health and Safety Executive, 2013c).

Unguarded machinery at a brewery

A worker lost two fingers when he attempted to clear a blockage in a grain dust extractor while it was still running. The Brewery, Hall and Woodhouse Ltd had moved the machinery into the building and workers in the building were to remove blockages from the machinery. It was argued that the brewery should have foreseen that workers would attempt to remove blockages whilst the machine was still working and were at risk of the moving parts. The Brewery was fined £6,000 and ordered to pay costs of £10,000 after they had pleaded guilty to breaching s.2(1) of the 1974 Act. A risk assessment of the machinery in the new location should have been carried out which would have identified this risk (Health and Safety Executive, 2013b).

Asbestos in an hotel

Britannica Hotels Ltd did not carry out a pre-work asbestos assessment prior to construction work at its hotel. When builders found the asbestos they called in a surveyor who found widespread asbestos which was removed by a licensed contractor. Asbestos causes serious lung disease but due to the latency of asbestosis the effect of exposure of both builders and guests is not known. The company was fined a total of £160,000 and ordered to pay £40,051 in costs (Health and Safety Executive, 2013e).

Measuring terms and rights

We can explore the application of discrimination legislation when we review terms and conditions. The primary employment terms in the contract are pay and benefits. Those responsible for reward management have to manage the legal and ethical risks of their financial decisions, and regardless of whether they manage to ensure this, it may not be viewed as sufficiently transparent as to seem legal and ethical to employees. This is important as the way in which the pay review is managed can influence the view employees have of the fairness of the organization, and any future claims, which are costly to the organization whether well founded or not.

Pay reviews

We have already looked at equal pay audits as a way of firstly monitoring equality and then removing inequality, but here we take a last view at monitoring equal pay as we also have the opportunity to ensure that pay is fair when it is reviewed annually. While many organizations may choose to make no increase to pay, or choose a percentage increase in line with the Consumer

Prices Index (CPI), collective pay reviews do not provide the opportunity to look at individual contributions. The pay review system is a business process in which we as HR professionals have an important role but is outside the scope of this book. However here we are looking at issues of measuring equality and resolving problems.

Pay reviews give us the opportunity to measure our pay against market rates and to deal with any inconsistency. However they also give us the opportunity to resolve any internal inconsistency, for example between genders. With smaller departmental pools of employees to review it is easier to see any discrepancies and resolve them, with reference to any information gathered from an equal pay audit. On a larger scale we also have the ability to use specialist modelling tools to illustrate the different outcomes for different pay increases and to measure the impact on people with particular protected characteristics.

Audits

Another way that we as HR professionals can protect our employer is to carry out an audit of particular areas. An audit is an evaluation of a process or system.

Recruitment and selection audit

We may review a process such as the recruitment and selection process to check that all paperwork that allows the employee to work has been gathered and is up to date. The scope of the audit depends on the time available and the importance of the information – it may be decided that it is necessary to check all employees, those recruited within the last five years or just a significant sample of the employees. The details of the accepted paperwork to prove an employee's right to work is covered in Chapter 4.

Auditing processes for reducing bribery

Another example of an audit would be evaluating the process for reducing or preventing bribery. Bribery is taking or giving a reward for acting dishonestly. In today's competitive world there is increasing pressure for employees to take steps that place their well-being first, and ethical, legal or moral positions are set at a lower priority. If the future of a deal places our position on a firmer footing, thus ensuring our family has the future we would wish, then as an employee we may be tempted.

The Bribery Act 2010 came into force in 2011 and s.7 makes it an offence, with an unlimited fine, for an organization to fail to prevent bribery, and those committing bribery face a punishment of up to 10 years in prison. This means that to protect the employer we need secure processes that prevent bribery. Whilst the details of the Act are too extensive to cover at this level, there is guidance provided by the Ministry of Justice (2011). There are six principles in the guide and procedures for anti-corruption should:

1 Be proportionate

2 Have top-level commitment

3 Have had a risk assessment carried out

4 Involve due diligence procedures

5 Be communicated and employees trained

6 Be reviewed and monitored.

When we discuss carrying out an audit of anti-corruption measures we are discussing principle 6 of the Ministry of Justice Guidance. For the HR professional it may be reviewing whistle-blowing policies and procedures, or policies on gifts, hospitality and expenses. Working with the finance department it may be necessary to audit expense claims. Working with the sales and marketing department we can review the effectiveness of any risk assessment form used and the effectiveness of bonus or commission in rewarding business yet acting to prevent corruption.

CASE STUDY   Bribing the clerk

There has been only one case that has applied the Bribery Act 2010. In *R. v Patel (Munir Yakub)* [2012] EWCA Crim 1243; [2013] 1 Cr. App. R. (S.) 48 a magistrate's court clerk was accused of taking bribes to allow people who had driving offences avoid prosecution. It was a prolonged and systematic breach of trust and the clerk was given four years' imprisonment, reduced to three years on appeal.

This does not mean that there were no previous bribery cases. In *Tesco Stores Limited v Simon Pook, Natasha Kersey Pook, Universal Projects (UK) Limited* [2003] EWHC 823 (Ch), false invoices were sent from Universal Projects (UK) Ltd to Tesco. Mr Pook was employed by Tesco in a senior and trusted position where he approved invoices, and so he was able to approve these invoices for £512,236. Tesco suggested that this was a bribe sent to the owner of Universal Projects (UK) Ltd. This argument was supported by the evidence and Tesco was able to reclaim the funds along with VAT from Mr Pook.

Public interest and a whistle-blowing policy

The Public Interest Disclosure Act 1998 governs whistle-blowing. This is a policy that protects the employer and so it is pertinent to provide a questionnaire to assess its effectiveness.

There have been some changes to the Public Interest Disclosure Act 1998 made in the summer of 2013, and these consist of the inclusion of disclosure being made in the public interest, and the removal of the need for disclosure to be made in good faith. Breaches in the person's own contract are not viewed as being made in the public interest, and should be made using the grievance procedure. Finally the employee who has made the disclosure is protected against detriment not only from the employer, but from adverse treatment from other employees.

FIGURE 7.1 Checklist: Whistle-blowing policy

	Yes	No
1. Does the policy provide a clear indication of those actions that the law states as unacceptable? These are:	☐	☐

- A criminal offence (s.43(1)(a))
- The breach of a legal obligation (s.43(1)(b))
- A miscarriage of justice (s.43(1)(c))
- A danger to the health and safety of any individual (s.43(1)(d))
- Damage to the environment (s.43(1)(e))
- Deliberate attempt to conceal any of the above (s.43(1)(f)).

	Yes	No
2. Does the policy provide a clear description of what the employer would believe is unacceptable?	☐	☐
3. Does the policy explain that the worker needs to believe that the disclosure is in the public interest?	☐	☐
4. Does the policy explain the sanctions for malicious disclosure?	☐	☐
5. Does the policy clearly explain that the employee should immediately tell their line manager?	☐	☐
6. Is it clear that they can also by-pass their line manager to report it to a more senior manager when appropriate?	☐	☐
7. Is it clear that all disclosures are in confidence and that the employee will not be put at a detriment for whistle-blowing?	☐	☐

Conclusion

We can measure the application of law to some degree by measuring the number of Employment Tribunal claims made against the employer. However we are aware that not all claims are well-founded and yet these cost the employer in legal advice and time spent gathering evidence and attending the Tribunal (or at times in settlement agreements). Not all unfounded claims are malicious; some are as a result of miscommunication, mistrust and lack of transparency. An employer must work within the law and must also be seen to work within the law.

We have considered a number of ways we can monitor the 'health' of the organization, and while some of these methods are internal to HR, others are more visible and can help communicate the commitment to working legally. The measurement of turnover and sickness absence in particular measure the employment relationship. Equality can be measured by checking pay reviews and equal opportunities monitoring. Reactive evaluation of accidents and incidents can be a preventative measure for future accidents. Finally audits can be carried out on all policies and procedures.

We finish this chapter by exploring changes in the Employment Tribunal system that may affect Employment Tribunal claims.

CASE STUDY   Developments in the Employment Tribunal system

The Employment Tribunals (Constitution and Rules of Procedure) Regulations 2013 (SI 2013/1948) has attempted to streamline the Employment Tribunal system and make it more flexible. This has resulted in a number of changes, some of which are discussed here.

The most radical change, and the one which has brought about most comment in the press, has been the use of fees for those making claims. 'Type A' claims are simple, uncomplicated claims such as unlawful deduction of wages or statutory redundancy payments. Claimants making 'Type A' claims will be charged £160 for making a claim and £230 for the hearing. 'Type B' claims will cover the majority of claims including unfair dismissal, discrimination and whistle-blowing. Claimants making 'Type B' claims will be charged £250 for making a claim and £950 for the hearing. (Costs are accurate for 2013.) There is a remission of fees for some claimants. It is not clear how this will affect Employment Tribunal claims. By October 2013, Unison and Fox Solicitors will have forced a judicial review of the fees. This means they will challenge the legality of fees as they believe the fees:

- offend against the principles of equivalence and effectiveness in European law;

- are indirectly discriminatory without justification;

- were made in breach of s.149 of the Equality Act 2010 (the public sector equality duty); and

- operate perversely in mass claims so as to raise revenue rather than to contribute towards costs.

Other changes to the process include amendments to Employment Tribunal claim forms (ET1) and response forms (ET3) and Initial Consideration of a claim by a Judge (after which it may be thrown out if there is no jurisdiction or no realistic prospect of success). Preliminary hearings have been simplified and during these a judge can:

- conduct a preliminary consideration of the claim with the parties and make a case management order;

- determine any preliminary issue;

- consider whether a claim or response, or any part, should be struck out under s.37;

- make a deposit order under s.39;

- explore the possibility of a settlement or alternative dispute resolution (including judicial mediation).

Finally costs orders (s.74), wasted time orders (s.80) and preparation time orders (s.76) have developed the ability for the successful party to receive some additional funds to cover costs in certain circumstances.

These changes along with early stage conciliation and settlement agreements have been put in place to reduce those cases going to Employment Tribunal (with costs for both parties), whilst attempting to provide justice for both parties. It is pertinent to remember that these changes are made at a time of economic hardship, when the cost of the Employment Tribunal Service is in question and businesses need support to compete. It is hoped that these needs have not superseded that of justice for all.

Conclusions and Government changes to employment law

08

We, as HR professionals, will firstly be called upon to interpret legislation to support line managers to carry out their business. But we will also need to use our legal knowledge to apply law to different options available to business managers. We can use our understanding to help businesses achieve their goals within current legal restrictions.

We have already discussed the challenging pace of change that business (and the HR professional) needs to meet. The changes below are indicative of the regular changes that we need to keep up to date with. Along with our up-to-date knowledge we need to apply a professional approach, recognizing the responsibilities of a HR professional and the requirements of the Chartered Institute of Personnel and Development (CIPD). We have a responsibility to support the employer to determine the choices that are right for the business, whilst maintaining its reputation, and some of our choices are not straightforward.

Changes to employment law

As a result of a continuing review of employment law there have been numerous changes, some of which will come into force early in April 2014. Many adaptations to employment law come about due to a change in Government and these proposed changes are no exception. It is difficult to predict the modifications that will be made after the initial promises to reduce red tape have been met. The focus of the Coalition Government has been to reduce restrictive employment laws to foster the green shoots of recovery, which in late 2013 are beginning to be seen. This of course also meets the political values of the Coalition Government and this leads us to recognize that changes to employment law are subject to changes in the political values of the Government in charge at the time. It is expected that the next election will be in 2015, with whoever is in power making future changes to employment law, which we, as HR professionals, will need to implement. So we can only predict possible changes to statute between 2013 and 2015.

We know already that pre-claim conciliation will have commenced by April 2014 with the aim of reducing Employment Tribunal claims. This is the most promising of a range of changes, particularly with regard to unfair dismissal. In practice we find that many Employment Tribunal claims are not easily settled and are often left to the last minute and many complicated and emotional cases will not settle. We can hope that pre-claim conciliation resolves more cases before Employment Tribunals but previous government intervention has not been successful, which is why pre-claim conciliation has been piloted and is now proposed.

Whilst there have already been some adaptations to whistle-blowing legislation through the Enterprise and Regulatory Reform Act 2013 there is currently a review of whistle-blowing legislation to be completed by November 2013. Whilst whistle-blowing provides a valuable method of identifying serious problems the Government has also identified cases where whistle-blowing did not occur, such as in the Mid-Staffordshire NHS Foundation Trust exposure (Department for Business, Innovation and Skills, 2013b). The Government is currently examining whether the law can be strengthened to support whistle-blowing and a response to the consultation will be published at the end of 2013.

One major change that will come into effect in April 2015 is the sharing of parental leave. It is proposed through the Children and Families Bill 2012–13, that a woman, after she has taken her compulsory maternity leave, will be able to share the remaining 50 weeks' leave with her partner, along with the remaining 37 weeks of maternity pay. In practice this will mean that a couple can take six months' leave together. The changes will also cover those who have adopted a child. The Bill also proposes to allow a partner to accompany a woman to ante-natal appointments and extends the right to request flexible working to all employees. The Children and Families Bill was heard in the House of Lords in the summer of 2013 and there may be some amendments before this Bill gains Royal Assent. The practical implications of the Bill for HR professionals will be challenging.

As at summer 2013 we are awaiting the judicial review of the Employment Tribunal fees according to the Employment Tribunals (Constitution and Rules of Procedure) Regulations 2013 (SI 2013/1948), mentioned in Chapter 7. Whether this, along with early conciliation and settlement agreements, will reduce the number of Employment Tribunal claims is not known. What is not in doubt, however, is that employment law will continue to change and remain complex and we as HR professionals will need to guide employers competently as they build their businesses.

The rationale of this book has not been to solely introduce new legislation but to introduce the HR professional to legislation. However it may be helpful for the reader to view both the extent of changes in 2013–14 and to determine where these are in the text and Table 8.1 provides this overview.

TABLE 8.1 Employment law changes

Chapter 1	• The inceptions of fees for Employment Tribunal claims • Early conciliation at Acas • Settlement agreements
Chapter 2	• None
Chapter 3	• None
Chapter 4	• Restricted certificate levels of sponsorship for 2013–14 • Proposed changes to the Transfer of Undertakings (Protection of Employment) Regulations 2006 • Changes to Universal Credit from 2013–2017 • The Health at Work Assessment and Advisory Service
Chapter 5	• Employee shareholder • Settlement agreements • The Health at Work Assessment and Advisory Service

TABLE 8.1 *continued*

Chapter 6	• None
Chapter 7	• Developments of the Employment Tribunal system • Changes to the Public Interest Disclosure Act 1998 made in the summer of 2013
Chapter 8	• Early conciliation • Changes to flexible working and parental leave • Whistle-blowing legislation • Inception of fees for the Employment Tribunal

REFERENCES AND FURTHER READING

Acas (2009a) [Accessed 29/09/13] Discipline and Grievance at Work: The Acas Guide [Online] http://www.acas.org.uk/media/pdf/s/o/Acas-Guide-on-discipline-and-grievances_at_work_%28April_11%29-accessible-version-may-2012.pdf

Acas (2009b) [Accessed 16/04/2013] Written Statement of Terms and Conditions of Employment [Online] http://www.acas.org.uk/index.aspx?articleid=3970

Acas (2010a) [Accessed 05/05/13] Job Evaluation: Considerations and Risks [Online] http://www.acas.org.uk/media/pdf/9/t/job-evaluation-considerations-risks-accessible-version-July-2011.pdf

Acas (2010b) [Accessed 20/04/2013] Varying a Contract of Employment [Online] http://www.acas.org.uk/media/pdf/8/6/Varying-a-contract-of-employment-accessible-version.pdf

Acas (2011) [Accessed 07/05/13] The Right to Apply for Flexible Working [Online] http://www.acas.org.uk/media/pdf/o/0/Right-to-apply-for-flexible-working-a-short-guide.pdf

Acas (2012a) [Accessed 18/04/2013] Transfer of Undertakings [Online] http://www.acas.org.uk/index.aspx?articleid=1655

Acas (2012b) [Accessed 16/04/2013] Workplace Snippets: The Benefits of a Diverse Workforce [Online] http://www.acas.org.uk/index.aspx?articleid=3725

Acas (2013a) Settlement Agreements: A Guide, Acas, London

Acas (2013b) Settlement Agreements: Code of Practice 4, Acas, London

Altman, M (2000) Labor rights and labor power and welfare maximization in a market economy: Revising the conventional wisdom, International Journal of Social Economics, 27(12), pp 1252–69

Arkin, A (1999) Return to Centre, People Management, 6 May, p 34

Armstrong, M (2012) Handbook of Human Resource Management Practice, 12th edition, Kogan Page, London

Aylott, E (2014) HR Fundamentals: Employee Relations, Kogan Page, London

Bass, B M (1985) Leadership and Performance Beyond Expectations, Free Press, New York

BBC (2008) [Accessed 15/06/13] Manchester: History Features [Online] http://www.bbc.co.uk/manchester/content/articles/2007/08/15/160807_peterloo_memorial_feature.shtml

Bies, R (2001) Interactional (In)justice: The sacred and the profane, in Greenberg, J and Cropanzano, R (eds), Advances in Organizational Justice, Stanford University Press, Palo Alto, CA

BIS – Department for Business, Innovation and Skills (2010a) [Accessed 29/07/13] Skills for Sustainable Growth [Online] https://www.gov.uk/government/news/a-new-vision-for-skills

BIS – Department for Business, Innovation and Skills (2010b) [Accessed 30/07/13] Work and Families Act 2006: Evaluation Report [Online] http://www.bis.gov.uk/assets/BISCore/employment-matters/docs/10-844-work-families-act-2006-evaluation.pdf

BIS – Department for Business, Innovation and Skills (2011a) [Accessed 16/04/13] Agency Workers Regulations: Guidance [Online] https://www.gov.uk/government/uploads/system/uploads/attachment_data/file/32121/11-949-agency-workers-regulations-guidance.pdf

BIS – Department for Business, Innovation and Skills (2011b) [Accessed 17/06/13] The Insolvency Service [Online] http://www.bis.gov.uk/insolvency/Redundancy/procedures

BIS – Department for Business, Innovation and Skills (2012) *Employment Law Review: Annual Update 2012*, HMSO, London

BIS – Department for Business, Innovation and Skills (2013a) *Employment Law 2013: Progress on Reform*, HMSO, London

BIS – Department for Business, Innovation and Skills (2013b) [Accessed 19/08/2013] The Whistle-Blowing Framework: Call for Evidence [Online] https://www.gov.uk/government/uploads/system/uploads/attachment_data/file/212076/bis-13-953-whistleblowing-framework-call-for-evidence.pdf

BIS – Department for Business, Innovation and Skills (2013c) [Accessed 29/09/2013] Transfer of Undertakings (Protection of Employment) Regulations 2006; Government Response to Consultation [Online] https://www.gov.uk/government/uploads/system/uploads/attachment_data/file/236932/bis-13-1023-transfer-of-undertakings-protection-of-employment-regulations-2006-government-response-to-consultation.pdf

Black, C and Frost, D (2011) *Health at Work: An independent review of sickness absence*, TSO, London

Blanchard, O and Landier, A (2002) The Perverse Effects of Partial Labour Market Reform: Fixed-term contracts in France, *The Economic Journal*, **112**, F214–F244

Bolton, T and Hughes, S (2001) *Absence Management*, Chandos Publishing, Oxford

Burns, J (1978) *Leadership*, Harper & Row, New York

CBI – Confederation of British Industry (2008) *Talent not Tokenism*, CBI, London

CBI – Confederation of British Industry (2010) [Accessed 27/07/2013] Making Britain the Place to Work [Online] http://www.cbi.org.uk/media/955580/2010.06-making_britain_the_place_to_work.pdf

Chartered Institute of Personnel and Development (2005) *Managing Diversity: People make the difference at work – but everyone is different*, Chartered Institute of Personnel and Development, London

Chartered Institute of Personnel and Development (2011) *Absence Management*, Chartered Institute of Personnel and Development, London

Chartered Institute of Personnel and Development (2012a) [Accessed 20/04/2013] A Guide to People Management when Preparing and Transferring Services [Online] http://www.cipd.co.uk/binaries/5745%20TUPE%20guide%20(WEB).pdf

Chartered Institute of Personnel and Development (2012b) *Absence Management*, Chartered Institute of Personnel and Development, London

Chartered Institute of Personnel and Development (2012c) [Accessed 18/06/13] Code of Professional Conduct [Online] http://www.cipd.co.uk/NR/rdonlyres/476C73A1-FBCD-4D08-A50E-2ACD31CF8E94/0/5740CodeofConduct.pdf

Chartered Institute of Personnel and Development (2012d) *Diversity in the Workplace: An overview*, Chartered Institute of Personnel and Development, London

Chartered Institute of Personnel and Development (2012e) [Accessed 17/06/2013] HR Business Partnering [Online] http://www.cipd.co.uk/hr-resources/factsheets/hr-business-partnering.aspx

Chartered Institute of Personnel and Development (2012f) [Accessed 27/07/2013] HR Professions Map: Our Professional Standards [Online] http://www.cipd.co.uk/binaries/HRPM%202%203.pdf

Chartered Institute of Personnel and Development (2012g) [Accessed 30/07/13] Succession Planning [Online] http://www.cipd.co.uk/hr-resources/factsheets/succession-planning.aspx

Chartered Institute of Personnel and Development (2013a) [Accessed 17/06/13] HR Outsourcing [Online] http://www.cipd.co.uk/hr-resources/factsheets/hr-outsourcing.aspx

Chartered Institute of Personnel and Development (2013b) [Accessed 16/08/13] Resourcing and Talent Planning Survey [Online] http://www.cipd.co.uk/hr-resources/survey-reports/resourcing-talent-planning-2013.aspx

Cohen, P N and Huffman, M L (2007) Working for the Woman? Female Managers and the Gender Wage Gap, *American Sociological Review*, **72**, pp 681–704

Collett, P (1999) *Exploring the Effects of Cultural Diversity at Work*, University of Oxford, Oxford

Cracknell, R (2010) [Accessed 13/04/13] *Key Issues for the New Parliament Briefing Paper: The ageing population* [Online] http://www.parliament.uk/documents/commons/lib/research/key_issues/Key%20Issues%20The%20ageing%20population2007.pdf

Creegan, C (2010) *Improving Sexual Orientation Monitoring*, Equality and Human Rights Commission, Manchester

Davis, P (2011) Economic Competitiveness and Employee Protections – a dichotomy?, *Human Resource Management International Digest*, **19**(6), pp 39–42

Davies, P (2013) [Accessed 29/07/13] Women on Boards [Online] https://www.gov.uk/government/uploads/system/uploads/attachment_data/file/182602/bis-13-p135-women-on-boards-2013.pdf

Deloitte Global Services (2011) [Accessed 29/07/2013] Women in the Boardroom: a Global Perspective [Online] http://www.deloitte.com/assets/Dcom-Tanzania/Local%20Assets/Documents/Deloitte%20Article_Women%20in%20the%20boardroom.pdf

Department for Work and Pensions (2012) [Accessed 20/04/13] Evaluation of the Fit to Work Service Pilots: First Year Report [Online] http://research.dwp.gov.uk/asd/asd5/rports2011-2012/rrep792.pdf

Department for Work and Pensions (2013a) [Accessed 29/09/2013] Fitness for Work: the Government response to the 'Health at Work – an independent review of sickness absence' [Online] https://www.gov.uk/government/uploads/system/uploads/attachment_data/file/181072/health-at-work-gov-response.pdf

Department for Work and Pensions (2013b) [Accessed 20/04/2013] Getting the Most Out of the Fit Note: Guidance for Employers and Line Managers [Online] http://www.dwp.gov.uk/docs/fitnote-employers-linemanagers-guidance.pdf

Doughty, S (2013) [Accessed 29/03/13] Number of workers taking disputes to tribunal falls by a fifth because of recession [Online] http://www.dailymail.co.uk/news/article-2264230/Number-workers-taking-disputes-tribunal-falls-fifth-recession.html

Equality and Human Rights Commission (2009a) [Accessed 29/07/13] Carrying Out an Equal Pay Audit [Online] http://www.equalityhumanrights.com/advice-and-guidance/tools-equal-pay/equal-pay-audit-toolkit/carrying-out-an-equal-pay-audit/

Equality and Human Rights Commission (2009b) [Accessed 29/07/13] Step 1: Additional Information [Online] http://www.equalityhumanrights.com/advice-and-guidance/tools-equal-pay/step-1-additional-information/

Equality and Human Rights Commission (2009c) [Accessed 29/07/13] Toolkit Step 2: Protected Group and Equal Work [Online] http://www.equalityhumanrights.com/advice-and-guidance/tools-equal-pay/toolkit-step-2-protected-groups-and-equal-work/

Equality and Human Rights Commission (2011a) [Accessed 29/07/13] Equal Pay: Statutory Code of Practice. [Online] http://www.equalityhumanrights.com/uploaded_files/EqualityAct/equalpaycode.pdf

Equality and Human Rights Commission (2011b) Equality Information and The Equality Duty: A Guide for Public Authorities, EHRC, Manchester

Esmail, A, Kaira, V and Abel, P (2005) A Critical Review of Leadership Interventions Aimed at People from Black and Minority Ethnic Groups, University of Manchester, Manchester

Eurofound (2009) [Accessed 15/06/2013] Job Evaluation Scheme [Online] http://www.eurofound.europa.eu/emire/UNITED%20KINGDOM/JOBEVALUATIONSCHEME-EN.htm

European Commission (2013) Tackling the Gender Pay Gap in the European Union, Publications Office of the European Union, Luxembourg

Freudenberger, H, Mather, F and Nardinelli, C (1984) A New Look at the Early Factory Labor Force, *The Journal of Economic History*, **44**(4), pp 1085–90

Financial Services Authority (2011) [Accessed 27/07/2013] About the Remuneration Code [Online] http://www.fsa.gov.uk/about/what/international/remuneration/about

Government Equalities Office (2011) [Accessed 12/05/13] Equality Act 2010: Practical Guide to Using Positive Action When Making Appointments [Online] https://www.gov.uk/government/uploads/system/uploads/attachment_data/file/85045/positive-action-practical-guide.pdf

Government Equalities Office (2012) Think, Act, Report: One Year On, HMSO, London

Gov.UK (2013a) [Accessed 13/04/13] Changes to the State Pension [Online] https://www.gov.uk/changes-state-pension

Gov.UK (2013b) [Accessed 15/06/2013] Minimum Ages Children can Work [Online] https://www.gov.uk/child-employment/minimum-ages-children-can-work

Gov.UK (2013c) [Accessed 05/05/13] Paternity Pay and Leave [Online] https://www.gov.uk/paternity-pay-leave/how-to-claim

Gov.UK (2013d) [Accessed 15/06/2013] Restrictions on Child Employment [Online] https://www.gov.uk/child-employment/restrictions-on-child-employment

Gov.UK (2013e) [Accessed 20/04/13] Simplifying the Welfare System and Making Work Pay [Online] https://www.gov.uk/government/policies/simplifying-the-welfare-system-and-making-sure-work-pays/supporting-pages/introducing-universal-credit

Gov.UK (2013f) [Accessed 20/04/13] Statutory Sick Pay [Online] https://www.gov.uk/statutory-sick-pay/eligibility

Gower, M and Hawkins, O (2013) [Accessed 13/04/13] Immigration and Asylum Policy: Government plans and progress made. SN/HA/5829 [Online] http://www.parliament.uk/briefing-papers/SN05829

The *Guardian* (2011) [Accessed 13/04/13] NHS Reform Live Blog – could you be a whistleblower? [Online] http://www.guardian.co.uk/society/blog/2011/jun/02/nhs-reforms-live-blog#block-5

Hansen, C D and Andersen, J H (2008) Going ill at Work – what personal circumstances, attitudes, and work-related factors are associated with sickness presenteeism?, *Social Science and Medicine*, **67**, pp 397–402

Hay Group (2005) [Accessed 09/06/2013] Hay Job Evaluation: Foundations and Applications Working Paper [Online] http://www.haygroup.com/downloads/ww/wp-Job_Evaluation.pdf

Hidden, A (1989) *Investigation into the Clapham Junction Railway Accident*, Department of Transport, HMSO, London

HMRC (n.d.) [Accessed 14/05/13] Employment Status Indicator [Online] http://www.hmrc.gov.uk/calcs/esi.htm

Holland, S (1996) The urgent need for a new deal for Europe, *European Labour Forum*, Winter 1996–1997, pp 5–9

House of Commons Treasury Committee (2009) [Accessed 27/07/13] Banking Crisis: Reforming corporate governance and pay in the City [Online] http://www.publications.parliament.uk/pa/cm200809/cmselect/cmtreasy/519/519.pdf

HSBC (2013a) [Accessed 02/04/13] Our Purpose [Online] http://www.hsbc.com/

HSBC (2013b) [Accessed 02/04/13] Our Purpose [Online] http://www.hsbc.com/citizenship/diversity-and-inclusion

HSE – Health and Safety Executive (1996) [Accessed 05/05/2013] Workplace, Health, Safety and Welfare, Workplace (Health, Safety and Welfare) Regulations 1992 Approved Code of Practice [Online] http://www.hse.gov.uk/pubns/priced/l24.pdf

HSE – Health and Safety Executive (2009) [Accessed 31/07/13] First Aid at Work; your questions answered [Online] http://www.hse.gov.uk/pubns/indg214.pdf

HSE – Health and Safety Executive (2013a) [Accessed 05/05/13] Birse Rail [Online] http://www.hse.gov.uk/business/casestudy/birserail.htm

HSE – Health and Safety Executive (2013b) [Accessed 09/08/2103] Brewery Fined After Worker Loses Two Fingers [Online] http://www.hse.gov.uk/press/2013/rnn-sw-hallwoodhouse.htm

HSE – Health and Safety Executive (2013c) [Accessed 09/08/13] Companies and Director Sentenced After Worker's Fatal Fall [Online] http://www.hse.gov.uk/press/2013/rnn-w-carillion-febrey.htm

HSE – Health and Safety Executive (2013d) [Accessed 06/05/13] Health and Safety Made Simple [Online] http://www.hse.gov.uk/simple-health-safety/index.htm

HSE – Health and Safety Executive (2013e) [Accessed 09/08/2013] Hotel Chain Fined for Asbestos Risk [Online] http://www.hse.gov.uk/press/2013/rnn-se-britannia.htm

HSE – Health and Safety Executive (2013f) [Accessed 15/06/13] Risk Assessment and Policy Template [Online] http://www.hse.gov.uk/risk/assessment.htm

Huczynski, A and Fitzpatrick, M (1989) *Managing Employee Absence for a Competitive Edge*, Pitman, London

Income Data Services (2011) *Equal Pay: Employment Law Handbook*, IDS, London

ILO – International Labour Organization (2013a) [Accessed 26/03/13] *Facts on Decent Work*, Switzerland, ILO [Online] http://www.ilo.org/wcmsp5/groups/public/--dgreports/--dcomm/documents/publication/wcms_082654.pdf

ILO – International Labour Organization (2013b) [Accessed 15/06/2013] Introduction to International Labour Standards [Online] http://www.ilo.org/global/standards/introduction-to-international-labour-standards/lang–en/index.htm

IOM – Institute of Occupational Medicine (n.d.) [Accessed 20/04/13] SART [Online] http://www.iom-world.org/sicknessabsence/devproj.htm

Kandola, R and Fullerton, J (1998) *Diversity in Action: Managing the mosaic*, Chartered Institute of Personnel and Development, London

Kerr, R and Robinson, S (2012) From Symbolic Violence to Economic Violence: The globalizing of the Scottish banking elite, *Organization Studies*, 33(2), pp 247–66

Kessler, R, Mickelson, K and Williams, D (1999) The prevalence, distribution and mental health correlates of perceived discrimination in the United States, *Journal of Health and Social Behavior*, **40**(3), pp 208–30

Kingsmill, D (2010) How to Pass the Baton, *Management Today*, **July**, p 24

Klaas, B S (2003) Professional Employer Organizations and Their Role in Small and Medium Enterprises: The impact of HR outsourcing, *Entrepreneurship: Theory and Practice*, **28**(1), pp 43–61

Kochan, T and Barocci, T (1985) *Human Resource Management and Industrial Relations*, Little Brown, Boston

Landau, P (2013) [Accessed 12/06/13] If you've got to go, negotiate a good settlement. Guardian.co.uk [blog] http://www.guardian.co.uk/money/work-blog/2012/jun/13/settlement-agreements-vince-cable

Leitch, S (2006) *Prosperity for All in the Global Economy: World class skills*, HMSO, Norwich

Leventhal, G S (1980) What should be done with equity theory?, in Gergen, K J, Greenberg, M S and Willis, R H (eds), *Social Exchange: Advances in theory and research*, Plenum, New York, pp 27–55

Local Government Group (2010) [Accessed 21/04/13] Health Work and Wellbeing in Local Authorities [Online] http://www.lge.gov.uk/lge/dio/8209418

London Councils (2013) [Accessed 09/06/2013] GLPC job Evaluation Scheme [Online] http://www.londoncouncils.gov.uk/committees/networks/reo/theglpcjobevaluationscheme.htm

M&S (2013) [Accessed 15/06/13] How We Do Business [Online] http://corporate.marksandspencer.com/howwedobusiness/our_policies/our_people

Majone, G (1993) The European community between social policy and social regulation, *Journal of Common Market Studies*, **31**(2), pp 153–70

Metz, I and Kulik, C (2008) Making Public Organisations More Inclusive: A Case Study of the Victoria Police Force, *Human Resource Management*, **47**(2), pp 369–87

Ministry of Justice (2011) [Accessed 10/08/13] The Bribery Act 2010: Guidance [Online] http://www.justice.gov.uk/downloads/legislation/bribery-act-2010-guidance.pdf

Ministry of Justice (2012) [Accessed 01/04/13] Employment Tribunals and EAT Statistics 2011–2012 [Online] http://www.justice.gov.uk/downloads/statistics/tribs-stats/employment-trib-stats-april-march-2011-12.pdf

Mullins, L (2010) *Management and Organisational Behaviour*, 9th edition, Pearson Education, Harlow

NHS Employers (2013) [Accessed 28/07/13] Health and Wellbeing Initiative [Online] http://www.nhsemployers.org/SharedLearning/Pages/Healthandwellbeinginitiative.aspx

NICE (2009) [Accessed 06/06/13] Managing Long Term Sickness and Incapacity for Work [Online] http://www.nice.org.uk/nicemedia/live/11779/43545/43545.pdf

Noh, S and Kaspar, V (2003) Perceived Discrimination and Depression: Moderating Effects of Coping, Acculturation and Ethnic Support, *American Journal of Public Health*, **93**(2), pp 232–38

OECD (1996) *Trade, Employment and Labour Standards: A study of core workers' rights and international trade*, OECD, Paris

OECD (2011) *Doing Better for Families*, OECD Publishing, Paris

Office for National Statistics (2013) [Accessed 12/04/13] Statistical Bulletin: Migration Statistics Quarterly Report February 2012 [Online] http://www.ons.gov.uk/ons/rel/migration1/migration-statistics-quarterly-report/february-2013/msqr-feb13.html#tab-2–Who-is-migrating-to-and-from-the-UK--

OSHCR (2013) [Accessed 14/06/2013] Occupational Safety and Health Consultants Register [Online] http://www.occupationalsafetyandhealthconsultantsregister.org/

Parliament UK (2013) [Accessed 15/06/13] Living Heritage: Reforming Society in the 19 Century [Online] http://www.parliament.uk/about/living-heritage/transformingsociety/livinglearning/19thcentury/overview/earlyfactorylegislation/

Personnel Today (2007) Legal Implications of Long-Term Absence for Employers and Occupational Health [Online] http://www.personneltoday.com/articles/05/10/2007/42410/legal-implications-of-long-term-absence-for-employers-and-occupational-health.htm

Pfeffer, J (1998) *The Human Equation: Building profits by putting people first*, Harvard Business School Press, Harvard

Pilbream, S and Corbridge, M (2010) *People Resourcing and Talent Planning: HRM in practice*, 4th edition, Pearson Education, Harlow

Pollert, A (2007) Britain and individual employment rights: paper tigers, fierce in appearance but missing in tooth and claw, *Economic and Industrial Democracy*, **28**(1), pp 110–39

Pollitt, D (2009) Hillingdon Council employees are healthy, happy... and here: Well-being package improves staff attendance, engagement and morale, *Human Resource Management International Digest*, **17**(7), pp 8–11

Poole, M (1980) Management strategies and industrial relations, in Poole, M and Mansfield, R (eds), *Managerial Roles in Industrial Relations*, Gower, London

Porter, M (1985) *Competitive Advantage*, Free Press, New York

Saridakis, G, Sen-Gupra, S, Edwards, P and Storey, D (2008) The Impact of Enterprise Size on Employment Tribunal Incidence and Outcomes: Evidence from Britain, *British Journal of Industrial Relations*, **46**(3), pp 469–99

Sellgren, K (2013) [Accessed 09/08/13] Many Mothers 'Feel Discriminated Against at Work' [Online] http://www.bbc.co.uk/news/education-23600465

Sockell, D (2013) [Accessed 27/07/13] Learning To Do the Right Thing, Right Now, Business Ethics [Online] http://business-ethics.com/2013/01/10/10545-learning-to-do-the-right-thing-right-here-right-now/

Stigler, G J (1946) The economics of minimum wage legislation, *American Economic Review*, **36**(3), pp 358–65

Sun, X (2002) How to Promote FDI? The Regulatory and Institutional Environment for Attracting FDI, in 4th Global Forum on Reinventing Government. Marrakesh, Morocco, 10–13 December 2002. Foreign Investment Advisory Service, Morocco

Syedain, H (2012) *Whistleblowers: You're next*, People Management, London

The *Telegraph* (2013) [Accessed 27/07/2013] Virgin Female Staff in 'Bra Wars' row over 'Skimpy' blouses that reveal dark underwear [Online] http://www.telegraph.co.uk/women/womens-life/10040922/Bra-wars-Virgin-female-staff-in-row-over-new-skimpy-blouses-that-reveal-dark-underwear.html

Tremlett, N and Banerji, N (1994) *The 1992 Survey of Industrial Tribunal Applications Great Britain*, Department of Employment, London

TUC (2011) [Accessed 13/04/2013] Unfair Dismissal Reform Will Leave Three Million Workers without Rights [Online] http://www.tuc.org.uk/workplace/tuc-19507-f0.cfm

TUC (2012) [Accessed 29/03/13] Cutting Redundancy Consultation Risks Increased Unemployment [Online] http://www.tuc.org.uk/workplace/tuc-20652-f0.cfm

Thomas, R (1992) Managing Diversity: A conceptual framework, in Jackson, S (ed), *Diversity in the Workplace*, Guildford Press, New York, NY

Thornhill, A, Saunders, M and Stead, J (1997) Downsizing, delayering – but where's the commitment? Development of a diagnostic tool to help manage survivors, *Personnel Review*, **26**(1/2), pp 81–98

UK Border Agency (2012a) [Accessed 13/04/13] Full Guide for Employers On Preventing Illegal Working in the UK [Online] http://www.ukba.homeoffice.gov.uk/sitecontent/documents/employersandsponsors/preventingillegalworking/currentguidanceandcodes/comprehensiveguidancefeb08.pdf?view=Binary

UK Border Agency (2012b) [Accessed 13/04/13] Quick Guide to the Points-Based System [Online] http://www.ukba.homeoffice.gov.uk/business-sponsors/points/quick-guide-pbs/

Ulrich, D and Brockbank, W (2008) The business partner model: 10 years on: lessons learned, *Human Resources Magazine*, **December 2008/January 2009**

Vinten, G (1998) Skills Shortage and Recruitment in the SME Sector, *Career Development International*, 3(6), pp 238–42

Waddell, G and Burton, A (2006) *Is Work Good for Your Health and Wellbeing?* The Stationery Office, London

Williams, D and Mohammed, S (2009) Discrimination and Racial Disparities in Health: Evidence and Needed Research, *Journal of Behavioural Medicine*, **32**, pp 20–47

Working Families (2013) [Accessed 09/08/13] Report on Working Families Legal Advice Service 2012 [Online] http://www.workingfamilies.org.uk/admin/uploads/Report%20of%20the%20helpline%202012%20%28Final%29%20for%20web.pdf

The World Bank (2011) [Accessed 01/04/13] Doing Business: Making a Difference for Entrepreneurs [Online] https://openknowledge.worldbank.org/handle/10986/2549

The World Bank (2012) [Accessed 01/04/13] Doing Business in a More Transparent World [Online] https://openknowledge.worldbank.org/bitstream/handle/10986/5907/DB12-FullReport.pdf?sequence=1

CASES AND LEGISLATION

Table of cases

Spencer (K) v Paragon Wallpapers [1976] IRLR 373

Spijkers v Gebroeders Benedik Abattoir CV (1986) ECR 1119

Süzen v Zehnacker Gebäudereinigung (1997) IRLR 255

Tarbuck v Sainsbury's Supermarkets Ltd [2006] IRLR 664

Taylor v Kent County Council (1969) 2 QB 560

Tesco Stores Limited v Simon Pook, Natasha Kersey Pook, Universal Projects (UK) Limited [2003] EWHC 823 (Ch)

Tower Hamlets LBC v Quayyum (1987) ICR 729

Walker v Northumberland County Council (1995) ICR 702 (QB)

William Hill Ltd v Tucker [1999] ICR 291

Legislation

If you want to read the original text of any acts, regulations, etc. then these can be found at:

www.legislation.gov.uk

A simple search facility allows you to access the legal text that you require.

INDEX